European Cities and Society

'*Much have I seen and known; cities of men*
And manners, climates, councils, governments . . . '

from Ulysses *by Alfred, Lord Tennyson*
(1809–1892)

for

ARTHUR KORN

with affection and gratitude

European Cities
and Society

**A Study of the Influence of Political
Climate on Town Design**

JAMES STEVENS CURL
Dip. Arch., Dip. T.P., M.R.I.A.I., A.R.I.B.A.

Leonard Hill · London
1970

Published by
Leonard Hill Books
A division of
International Textbook Company Ltd
158 Buckingham Palace Road, London S.W.1

First Published 1970
ISBN 0 249 43994 8

Printed in Great Britain by
W. S. Cowell Ltd, at the Butter Market, Ipswich

Contents

List of Figures

Chapter I

1. Biosphere and Noösphere: typology
2. Mandala forms
   Vitruvian Man (after Leonardo da Vinci)
   Sforzinda (after Filarete)
   Vitruvian Ideal City
3. Ideal Cities (Mandala Variants)
   Ideal City (after Lorini)
   Ideal City (after Cataneo)
   Ideal City (after Scamozzi)
4. Mandala forms
   Labyrinths
   Palma Nova
   Ideal City (after Martini)

Chapter II

5. Ur (*c.* 2000 B.C.) (after Woolley and Banister Fletcher)
6. Babylon (after Breasted and others)
7. Necropolis (after Banister Fletcher and other sources)
   Pyramids and Sphinx
   Pyramid at Sakkara
8. Walls as dominants
   Tiryns and Mycenae (after Banister Fletcher)

Chapter III

9. Athens in the Fifth Century, B.C. (after various sources)
10. Plan of Priene (after various sources)
11. Plan of Miletus (after Wycherley, R. E., and others)
12. Alexandria (after various sources, especially map in
    Cities of Destiny, p. 113 (see Bibliography))
13. Pergamon: the upper city (after various sources)

Chapter IX—*cont.*

All Figures were drawn by the author. Sources are given, but where it is stated that the sources are 'various', then it is to be understood that the sketches or places have been adapted, salient points having been taken from several originals.

List of Plates

All plates are from photographs by the author, taken over the period 1959–1968, with the exceptions of plates 21, 22, 50–55 which are from the Mansell Collection, plates 111 and 112 which are from *National Evils and Practical Remedies with the Plan of a Model Town* by James S. Buckingham (see Bibliography), and plates 122–126 which are from *Neue Deutsche Baukunst* (see Bibliography).

Preface and Acknowledgements

Since I first began collecting material for this book, much of what has delighted me in the fabric and detail of the cities I have known and loved has been either destroyed or spoiled. Forces of widespread philistinism have been at work, armed with words such as 'progress', 'development', 'modernization' and other utterances, which depend entirely on the value-judgement of contemporary understanding of them: in actual fact these words have, for the most part, been used to justify more destruction of the environment than even past wars achieved. There is, however, a glimmer of hope for those who hold visual quality dear: questions are in the air, and clearly a new generation of designers is reacting against the so-called 'functionalism' and 'empiricism' of a decade or two ago. Clearly the sheer boredom of so much of our environment has been responsible for a new movement which may be gaining ground. Appreciation of Baroque art and *Art-Nouveau*, among others, would indicate that a hankering after more sensual things is latent in us all, especially after a period of clinical dullness.

Environment on a large scale is ordered by dominant groups in a society, and this book is an attempt to show how the ruling social classes expressed themselves in the dominants of cities. Necessarily, it must only be a selective series of studies, covering only areas which express the main stream of Western European city development, linked chronologically, and by the thread of the concept of political climate *vis-à-vis* town design.

It is my conviction that Mankind will and must continue to live in Cities, for it is only in Cities, as the Greek philosophers knew, that all the facets of civilized life may be found. Cities, however, must be splendid places in which to live, and since it is clear that the dominant forces at work are anti-City, in that their roads and office blocks are carving the Cities into meaningless pieces, then they must be recognized as monstrous enemies of a truly cultured society. Some argue for armed revolution, while others would opt for more subtle methods aimed at a constant outpouring of ideas which, if strong enough and often enough declaimed, will gradually change the political climate. We therefore must create enough models of reality, and make sure they are truly based on the acceptance of the wholeness of life, so that they become reality itself. A model of reality not only *expresses* but *creates* reality, for Auschwitz and Buchenwald were not only the product of a *Zeitgeist*, but they were the models which helped to mould a reality, and they became themselves the last, dreadful reality. The current cry for more specialization, more systems, more technology, especially in city design, would indicate that it is not understood that a totality of vision rather than a growth of more compartmentalization is what is needed. A system unguided by a totality of philosophical content with its roots in all human experience, ends up producing an Auschwitz or its spiritual equivalent. Specialization is the greatest danger, in my opinion, to contemporary life. In the words of John Donne: *No man is an Island, entire of itself; every man is a piece of the Continent, a part of the main. . . . Any man's death diminishes me, because I am involved in Mankind; And therefore never send to know for whom the bell tolls; it tolls for thee.* (Devotions, XVII.)

This book has necessarily had to draw facts and opinions from hundreds of sources as well as from my own experiences, observations and ideas. I have tried to give as full a Bibliography as possible to augment the book, and I have acknowledged sources wherever possible, but, in a work of this nature, it is difficult to know what concepts, now so much a part of me, emanated from other people or from my own mind. We all inter-relate, and I am especially grateful to those whose ideas may be here but which are now so much a part of my own philosophy that I cannot tell from whence they came. I acknowledge my debt to all those friends, acquaintances and casual encounters who gave me hospitality in my travels, talked far into the nights with me in many cities and towns, and simply gave and took, in short, communicated with me.

I am grateful to Routledge and Kegan Paul, Ltd., for permission to quote from *The Ideal City in its Architectural Evolution* by Helen Rosenau and *The West European City* by R. E. Dickinson; to Messrs. Bowes and Bowes for permissions relating to Erich Heller's *The Disinherited Mind*; to Mr. R. E. Thomas of Princeton University Press; to Cassell and Co. Ltd., for permission to use some material in *The Jackdaw of Linz* by David Roxan and Ken

Wanstall; to Longmans, Green and Co. Ltd., for permissions relating to *A Prospect of Cities* by Cecil Stewart; to Macmillan and Co. Ltd., in connection with R. E. Wycherley's *How the Greeks Built Cities*; to Martin Secker and Warburg Ltd., and Harcourt, Brace and World Inc., for permissions to quote from Lewis Mumford's *The Condition of Man* and *The Culture of Cities*; to J. M. Dent and Sons Ltd., and E. P. Dutton and Co. Inc., for permissions in connection with Plato's *The Republic* tr. A. D. Lindsay, Plato's *The Laws* tr. A. E. Taylor, and Aristotle's *Politics* tr. John Warrington, all Everyman's Library editions; to Percy Lund, Humphries and Co. Ltd., for permission to quote from Arthur Korn's *History Builds the Town*.

I acknowledge my indebtedness to *Cities of Destiny*, ed. Toynbee, published by Thames and Hudson. Thanks are also due to The Athlone Press of the University of London for permission to adapt illustrations from *A History of Architecture on the Comparative Method* by Sir Banister Fletcher.

I also wish to thank Sir Frederic Osborn; the Editor of *Town and Country Planning*; the Editor of the *Architectural Review*; Nicholas Taylor; the Herr Direktor, Dr. Wacha, of the Stadtmuseum, Linz; Dr. Kraiting, of the Presse and Informationsamt der Bundesregierung; the Librarian of the Town Planning Institute; the Librarian of the Literary and Philosophical Society, Newcastle-upon-Tyne; Herr Architekt Albert Speer and Arthur Korn, who kindly permitted me to dedicate this book to him.

I should also like to record my appreciation of the interest shown in my work by Sigfried Giedion, who was kind enough to write to me expressing the hope that he would be able to read the book after publication. I very much regret his death in 1968.

I especially wish to thank all those friends who talked over so many ideas with me and accompanied me on marathon walks in search of the past, of the present, and of glimpses into the future. I owe a great debt of gratitude to all those in past times who created so much of beauty in the urban environment, for it has been a pleasurable task collecting material. I am very grateful to my father, George Curl, who read over the proofs for me.

Finally, I thank Mary Lane, who typed the manuscript so well; and Rodney Roach, who helped with the enlargement of the photographs.

James Stevens Curl
Oxford 1970

I

Introduction and Definitions

This book attempts to show that political climate has always influenced the design of major urban settlements. The scope of the study is confined to the antique civilizations which have had a traceable effect on the developing European cultures, and to those cultures themselves considered up to the present day. Whilst use is made of the conventional chronological divisions of the history of the various periods, occasional overlapping and cross-reference is unavoidable. For reasons of compactness, most of the towns discussed are European, but a few examples from other non-European cultures are mentioned where relevant to the subject.

THE ARGUMENT

The argument, briefly, is that the political climate is determined by the dominant members of a society, that is, by the ruling classes, and that the political climate thus created in turn influences the design of urban settlements profoundly. It will be demonstrated that the aspirations of the ruling classes, and indeed their qualities, are reflected in the 'inscape' of a town, and, in the case of many cultures, by the actual shape of the town plan.

SOME DEFINITIONS

Political Climate
'Political climate', as meant here, may be defined as the prevailing mood of a society as determined by its ruling elements, i.e. the groups holding political power. It will be the complex of opinion prevalent at a particular time that influences the policies of a society.

'Political' is that which is pertaining to parties differing in their views of government. 'Climate' is the character of something or its condition. Perhaps the word that best expresses what is meant in this study by 'political climate' is the German term 'Zeitgeist'.

This is composed of two words: 'Zeit', meaning 'time', and 'Geist', meaning 'spirit' or 'prevalent mood'.

Paul Kriesis states[1] that if the political climate in which a citizen lives can be assessed correctly, and if we can form a true insight into his reactions and attitudes to a situation, we should be able to predict the development of future city centres and also the settlement form.

Town and City

Definitions of the terms 'town' and 'city' have been attempted by many, including Le Corbusier, who stated that 'a town is an object for use'.

Geddes suggested that towns are divided into those functions serving production, those serving distribution, and those providing residential, recreational and educational facilities. These he described as primary, secondary and tertiary functions.

Max Weber said it was wrong to speak of 'the town', but that it was correct to talk of particular towns or types of town. That a town is an 'urban community' would seem to be a reasonable statement, but again it lacks a specific interpretation of the meaning of the term.

Arthur Korn states[2] that 'the town is a social phenomenon'. He goes on to say that its growth and structure are determined by nature in a broad sense, and by the level of technique and the organization possessed by society.

While agreeing with many of the definitions above, I would attempt to define a town as a more or less closely grouped collection of buildings housing different functions, and the more diversified and mixed the functions, the more lively the town will be. The level of sophistication possessed by a town will ultimately depend upon the degree of culture, in its widest sense, acquired by the politically dominant citizens of a town. A town is essentially *the urban habitat of civilized man, the nature of which is a combination of functions needed in the service of a society that has aspirations towards sophistication.* Urban character is usually found when these functions are discovered together, are organized into physical structures and form a cohesion. Such places with urban qualities vary greatly in status and in character, and so various terms are used to describe

[1]   In an article entitled Metropolitan Centres in the *Architects' Year Book*, No. 9, p. 61.
[2]   In *History Builds the Town* p. 3.

them at different times in history. It must be stressed that each urban function requires particular structures or elements of form.[1]

R. E. Dickinson[2] has given us an exhaustive account of the origins and nature of the urban habitat. According to Dickinson, the term 'civitas' originally signified a district of organization under the Romans, but was later transformed during the Merovingian and Carolingian Empires to the centre of an area in which was a bishopric. This nucleus in France became a 'cité'. By the twelfth century, the term 'civitas' referred to a settlement that had a special law, that had a wall and that was a marketing, industrial and commercial centre. The word denoted a settlement no matter if it were large, like Paris, or if it were merely a local centre, for it was outstanding in its functions, laws and also in its physical form. 'Civitas' became the 'ville' of France, the 'Stadt' of Germany, and the 'town' of England.[1] The term 'cité' or 'city' originally signified the ecclesiastical centre, and it is still used in this sense in France and in England. Other less significant settlements had rudimentary defences, only basic laws, and occasionally held markets: these were the 'market towns', 'bourgs' or 'Flecken'.

The city, in a wider modern sense, is a major centre for institutions, administration and organization, cultural life, social contact, production, commercial activity and transport, as well as being a place for the residence and work of the various citizens from all strata of society. It may have pleasurable aspects too, where the amenities of urban life may be enjoyed. It may perhaps be a political capital or a great centre for the arts.

Lewis Mumford states[3] that the city is the 'point of maximum concentration for the power and culture of a community.' In the wonderful Introduction to *The Culture of Cities*, he draws our attention to the fact that the city is not only the form but the *symbol* of an integrated social relationship, and that it acts like a lens, to focus all the rays of the separated activities of life, so that they become significant and whole. Mumford also reminds us that cities arose out of social needs, and in return they magnify the means of expression of such needs.

Functions combine, decline, emerge and grow at different times to give new emphasis and new characteristics to a city.

---

[1] See *The West European City* Chapter 14.
[2] See *The West European City* pp. 251–278.
[3] In *The Culture of Cities* p. 3.

Dr. Helen Rosenau[1] quotes Aristotle's remark in *Politics* that 'A Citie is a perfect and absolute assembly or communion of many townes or streets in one,'[2] which is as fair comment as any. Dr. Rosenau's work will be mentioned later in this study in connection with the vision of ideal cities.

Imageability and Inscape

In his book *The Image of the City*, Kevin Lynch has developed the concept of 'imageability' in reference to all kinds of features which make a strong impression on memory.[3] A highly 'imageable' city, according to Lynch, would appear very remarkable, so that it would encourage the person so affected to greater 'attention and participation'. Lynch stresses that 'imageability' is sensuous in quality, and imparts delight or some other positive reaction to the person experiencing the city with such a virtue. Venice springs to mind as a city with 'imageability'. Amsterdam, Delft, Haarlem, parts of London, Paris and Vienna, to name but a few, undoubtedly possess it. Mr. Carver[4] points out that 'imageability' may depend on trivia, prominent buildings or even on some quality or feeling in a district of a city. The term 'inscape' was used by Gerard Manley Hopkins to define a quality in an object seen which could excite him to produce poetry. Carver uses the term 'inscape' to denote the genius loci of a city: some quality which cannot be defined; which moves one to emotional involvement with a place in a positive way. Mr. Carver puts it beautifully when he contrasts such an impact upon 'the heart and mind' with some other situation or place which leaves 'a deposit upon the memory'.

Taking the concept further, and accepting 'imageability' and 'inscape' as valid terms, we then must ask ourselves why some cities and towns have both qualities whereas others possess neither. This lack of inscape is particularly noticeable in much of the new development throughout our civilization. I would suggest that there is a very good reason for this. We know a great deal about water supply, sewage disposal, traffic, economics, the working and leisure habits of the people, new and traditional building methods, layouts, densities, and so on. What is forgotten, however, is that in the sphere of catering for people and their environmental needs, the sphere is

---

[1] In *The Ideal City* p. 3.
[2] From a translation of 1598.
[3] See *The Image of the City* pp. 9-13.
[4] Humphrey Carver, in *Cities in the Suburbs* p. 20.

composed of shades of emphasis: the Biosphere and the Noösphere. We know much about the former, but we refuse, apparently, to recognize even the existence of the latter. Now these two shades of emphasis are part of a whole, and the spiritual, mental, soulful part – call it what you will – is practically ignored when new development takes place. In the nineteenth century, reformers finally obtained pure drinking water for the urban masses, efficient sewage disposal, and certain minimum constructional standards after a long struggle. The fight for the Biosphere has progressed some way, but the champions of the Noösphere have a long way to go before the two parts balance, and an entity is restored.

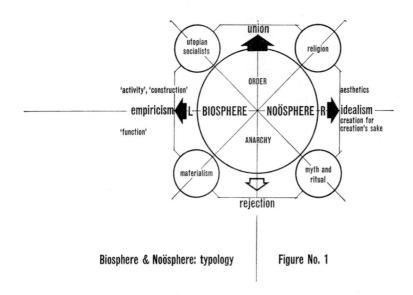

Biosphere & Noösphere: typology | Figure No. 1

The typology suggested is merely diagrammatic. The large circle must be imagined as a sphere, and it consists of a whole spectrum of mood and *nuance*. It is only possible to give a small basic direction idea of the opposing forces within the totality. Clearly, the empiricist, in his 'purest' form, will reject any idealism, because it is not measurable, and so his data will be suspect, not on empiricist grounds, but within the larger context of reality. His analysis of a problem, therefore, will be incomplete, and must result in the wrong answer, since he will have ignored a considerable number of the factors because they are not measurable or because he has not evolved techniques to measure them. Some kind of catalyst must be found to bring the forces together so that a synthesis may be achieved, or a union, as I have shown. It must be emphasized that a diagram in two dimensions cannot do anything but *suggest* the idea.

The Mandala

M.-L von Franz has explained[1] that the circle or sphere is a symbol of self. They embody and symbolize the totality of the psyche in all its aspects, including the relationship between man, the universe and nature. In eastern religions this relationship is graphically represented: e.g. the image of Brahma is seen standing on a thousand petalled lotus, turning his eyes to the cardinal points of the compass, and this stance is known as 'primary orientation'.

In Zen Buddhist teaching, the circle represents enlightenment and perfection and the circle divided into eight represents the entire cosmos in its relationship to divine powers. This circular form, with basic sub-divisions from the centre of the circle, is known as a mandala form and is interpreted in Jungian terms as an archetypal image from within the human unconscious. It is significant that the mandala is found in so many Utopian designs for the ideal city such as Palma Nova, Saarlouis, and even Ebenezer Howard's 'garden city'.[2]

The mandala as a circular form is seen as the awakener and preserver of life. The way in which it is combined with other figures, however, may give prominence to one meaning or another. As Giedion points out,[3] 'the total significance of circular forms cannot be confined within the bounds of exact definition.'

The renaissance Masters merged all consciousness into a new ordered coherence of pattern based on mandala forms. Mr. Humphrey Carver suggests in an excellent diagram[4] that renaissance man 'imposed his own dimensions and ideals upon the total form of the city'. And what heroic dimensions they were! It is readily seen that a city designed on the mandala form becomes a symbol of psychic wholeness and exerts a specific influence on the people living there. This is a fundamental point in the argument, for the political climate will, by its very nature, be expressed as a symbol

[1] In *Man and his Symbols*.
[2] See *The Ideal City* Plates II and VI and Figs. 5, 9, 10 and 14. See also *Garden Cities of Tomorrow* pp. 52, 53 and 143.
[3] In *The Eternal Present* Vol. I, p. 125.
[4] In *Cities in the Suburbs* p. 31.

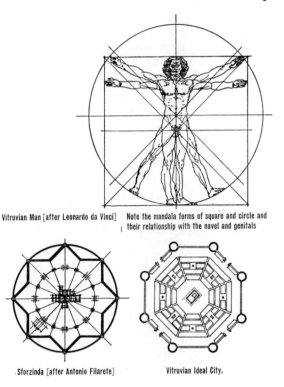

Vitruvian Man [after Leonardo da Vinci]   Note the mandala forms of square and circle and their relationship with the navel and genitals

.Sforzinda [after Antonio Filarete]   Vitruvian Ideal City.

Mandala forms   Figure No. 2

in the town design, either in the form of the plan or in the dominant elements in the physical structure.

Symbol and Allegory
Towards the end of the Middle Ages, a tremendous change in ideas of reality occurred, culminating in the theological arguments of Luther and Zwingli. For Luther, a symbol was not only a pictorial representation of something, but it was that something itself. In this view, Luther demonstrated that he was essentially a man of the mediaeval period, steeped in its intellectual processes and in the fundamentals of its thought. Ulrich Zwingli, on the other hand, was more of a man of the renaissance. For him a symbol was mostly a representation of something which it itself was not. Although the symbols in question were those of the Eucharist, the change of intellectual attitudes to symbols was a profound revolution in its day.

Ideal City [after Lorini]

Ideal City [after Cataneo]

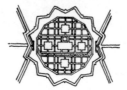

Ideal City [after Scamozzi]

Ideal Cities [mandala variants]   Figure No. 3

The Renaissance, with the ensuing worship of reason, relegated the symbol to a very minor position in the lives of men, for reality became real in itself, and was freed from the mysteries of the symbol. As the symbol declined in significance, so reality lost its symbolic meanings, and even God became remote from everyday affairs. The union of image and object, bread and body, Biosphere and Noösphere was ruptured. Attempts were made to reunite the two facets, notably by the English metaphysical poets, who seem to express a deep mystic longing for a reunion with the symbols which had been robbed of their meaning. In this study, an attempt is made to regard the symbol as such, and not as an allegory. A marble maiden emptying a vase of wine on the ground is an allegory of Temperance. An allegory, therefore, for the purposes of this book, is an abstraction, while a symbol is something specific. The symbol for Goethe,

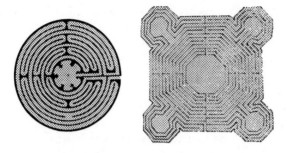

Pilgrimage or Grail symbols from the Middle Ages. Such labyrinths were depicted in the floors of Cathedrals either as individual tiles or as real ways of prayer such as at Rheims [above]

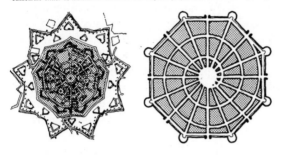

Palma Nova: the Venetian fortress town   Ideal City [after Martini]

Mandala forms   Figure No. 4

and for Nietzsche too, was real. Nietzsche described it as the 'language of the universal.'[1]

Historical Imagination
This study must inevitably involve the consideration of power and the social order of the day contributing to the Zeitgeist. Historically speaking, conventional studies will reveal quantities of what pass as facts, but in the present investigation, something more is involved, namely, the seeking of the quality of the political climate at particular periods and how it affected the inscape and imageability of

[1] *The Disinherited Mind* p. 95.
There is a magnificent exposition of the differences between the symbol and the allegory in an essay by Heller called *The Hazard of Modern Poetry*, pp. 227–257 in the same volume.

towns and cities. We are seeking the Geist which left its mark on the physical form of the urban habitat.

Now in order to attempt to recapture the essence of the Zeitgeist of another age, historical research is, of course, essential, but sensibility and intuition must play their parts. An examination of this kind must have a critical method differing from the techniques of, say, an architectural history considered purely in terms of form. In a sense, we must feel a kind of creative sympathy for a culture in order to enter into its essential mood, which was, of course, the Zeitgeist,[1] and which was the atmosphere in which towns and cities were created, added to or grew. This point must be stressed, for it is only in comparatively recent years that architectural historians have started to look upon the baroque and rococo periods with sympathy. We are therefore forced to the conclusion that, since those periods were generally held in low repute only a few years ago, fashion plays a greater part than so-called 'objectivity' in architectural criticism. This is where creative sympathy and historical imagination are indispensable, to enable us to attempt to feel the Zeitgeist of a period so that we can view contemporary developments with a less cloudy eye.

Other dangers lie in wait for us, for not only have we lost the language of symbols, but we have built up a belief in the power and scope of what our age thinks are objective criteria for criticism. The concepts of our time constantly mislead us. Ideas which are used freely by critics, writers, the press and politicians, and which are charged with emotive and over-used terms, may, in fact, be assessments of values which are tainted with cant, dishonesty and the prejudices of our understanding of affairs. The explosiveness in words such as 'race', 'bourgeoisie', 'democracy' or 'slavery', for example, when trying to discuss a period in history, may render the exercise useless and understanding impossible unless historical imagination is used, for the scales of value will always change as there are no absolutes. A 'free' citizen with voting rights may approach a greater degree of slavery than did a mediaeval serf, a Greek slave, or even an eighteenth century worker, depending on the scale of values applied.

Creative minds, endowed with vision, lead the way to social change, while social change, in turn, alters the vision of artists as well as the tastes of those under whose patronage the artist can

---

[1]   See *Essay on Burckhardt and Nietzsche* in *The Disinherited Mind*.

function. Clearly, works of art symbolize the Zeitgeist. Marxists hold that it is the social being of men that determines their consciousness, and not their consciousness that determines their social being. I disagree with this view, and believe that there is an interaction, so that both statements are true. The will to change, strive and create, and the daemonic forces within man have been underestimated in contemporary observations, as the traditions of empiricism and reason have held sway, and the Noösphere has been ignored. There is no dogma which can be completely true, for the complexities of life are such that everything must interact and influence everything else. Striving after something noble, great, beautiful, something ideal, has been a feature of many cultures, and has found expression in philosophy, art, religion, architecture, literature, poetry, music, and the design of towns. This struggle, when applied to man himself, in a seeking to better his own intellectual and moral stature, was expressed by Nietzsche, and converted by some mysterious process to a popular belief that Nietzsche preached a new religion which gave the green light to violence, murder and complete ruthlessness, clearly a complete misunderstanding of his philosophy.

Notions of what is and what is not economically or practically feasible have obviously played little part in such a struggle for the qualities of an ideal. In Marxist terms this is because the dominant elements of a society not only influence, but control the mass, sometimes referred to as the *base*, while the dominants are described as the *superstructure*.

A swing to Idealism usually appears during times of great social changes, or impending changes, when the decline of existing orders quickens the search for new modes of expression and encourages experiments in the creative field. Such new expressions together with intellectual experiment usually act in opposition to the Establishment, and thus the decline of existing orders is hastened. Utopian ideas reflect the searchings of the leading minds of a civilization, and usually express the longing to impose order where there is chaos. They may, in fact, be the striving for answers to problems which may only be transitory, but their very existence is significant, for they are an attempt to change, and for this very reason they not only shed light on existing social orders, but they threaten them as well.

II

The Antique Civilizations

INTRODUCTION: THE RIVER CULTURES

The siting of ancient cultures was in great river valleys liable to natural flooding such as those of the Nile, the Indus, the Tigris and the Euphrates. The economic basis of these cultures was decided by irrigation, which was carried out by a peasant class using palaeo-technic methods much dependent on manpower. The river had a unifying effect, linking isolated regions by acting as the main artery for transport and commerce as well as for life itself. A river, forced by politicians into becoming a boundary, is in a very curious state, for river valleys have characters and cultures of their own which do not vary from bank to bank. Cultures may differ along the *length* of the river, but not across it. For example, Upper and Lower Egypt were at war for many years until they were finally united by military conquest. About 3000 B.C. the war between the Two Lands was ended when the Upper Egyptian King Na'r defeated the forces of the Delta. If a river becomes a political boundary after the river valley settlements have developed naturally, towns may decay and die because they may be split down the middle, or, if they are built on one bank only, cut off from half their natural 'umland' and hinterland. Around a centre such as a town, an 'urban field' exists. Part of this area will be intimately associated with the daily life of the centre. This intimately associated area is termed an *umland*. Large centres develop distinct umlands beyond which is a wider area where most social, commercial and service contacts are made between the country and the smaller towns, while specialized needs are catered for in the centre. This wider area is known as the *hinterland*.[1]

---

[1] For further information on the 'urban hierarchy' and 'urban fields' see *The City Region in Western Europe* pp. 47–59 and 194–198.

MESOPOTAMIA

As far as is at present known, Sumer was the first area in which cities were built in any significant numbers. The basin of the rivers Tigris and Euphrates supported a number of Sumerian city-states: these must have been created with great organization of labour, for not only were walled cities built, but swamps and jungles were made into canals and fields. Although the Sumerian city-states shared a common cultural root, when their energies had cleared the jungles, drained the swamps, and organized irrigation complexes, their territories began to touch and even overlap, so that frontier disputes caused inevitable friction. War between Sumerian city-states appears to have been frequent, violent and destructive, so that, in time, one state emerged victorious.[1] The establishment of the Sumerian empire gave peace, but it was a costly peace in terms of destruction, misery and loss of life. Arnold Toynbee, in his introduction to the book *Cities of Destiny*, draws our attention to the similarity of Sumerian developments to Graeco-Roman civilization, pre-Columbian Middle America and China in this respect.

Sumeria was invaded by Amorites, and, about the end of the third millenium B.C., Babylon was founded. The traditions of warfare in the cultures of Sumer and Akkad created strong military organizations, converting princely rulers who were victorious into warlords, and their palaces into the centres of political and military power. Strong fortifications were developed.[2] The small area of the states of Sumer and Akkad seems first to have achieved unity and peace under a Semitic king, then under the kings of Ur, and finally, under Hammurabi of Babylon (*c.* 2250 B.C.). Hammurabi was an Amorite himself, and although his régime did not last, his city of Babylon did, and became the imperial capital that Ur had failed to become. For fifteen hundred years, Babylon was the capital of many empires which had their economies based on the trade of foodstuffs from the fertile basin of the rivers.

The first monumental dominants in cities were, as far as we know, temples. These were undoubtedly symptoms of attempts to contact forces outside man himself, for it is only much later in the history of Mesopotamian religion that images appear which are human in form, and these images usually date from the time of the rise of kings

---

[1] *Cities of Destiny* pp. 14 and 15.
[2] *History Builds the Town* p. 20.

to despotic power. The most tremendous expressions of monumental dominants are the ziggurats of Mesopotamia and the pyramids of Egypt. They are the products of a dominant ruling class and also the 'expression and symbol of contact established . . . with the superhuman forces'.[1]

The ziggurat was built within cities as a stepped tower with a temple on the top. This temple was accessible from the temple precinct at ground level and was dedicated to the god of the city, although the common people were probably denied access to the summit. The temple was the house of a god, and could be seen from the ground, so visual contact was maintained between deity and people. The ziggurat, therefore, was part of the physical structure as well as the organic whole of the city. It essentially *belonged* and was involved in daily life. In the classic period of the ziggurat, at Ur, for example, the most important architecture, such as the house of the king, the priestly dwellings and the treasury, all stood near the ziggurat and were dwarfed by it. In other words, the ziggurat was the architectural dominant of the city, and expressed the political power wielded by the priesthood through their contact with a supernatural force. Throughout the history of Mesopotamia, the ziggurat was the central symbol of a religion, and was venerated by Sumerians, Akkadians, Babylonians and Assyrians alike.[2]

The ziggurat and the pyramid both derive from a striving towards the heaven in an architectural form as a symbol of reaching the gods. In the ziggurat, symmetrical stairs leading to the summit, strangely reminiscent of the temple bases of Aztec Mexico, formed enormous processional ways for the priesthood. The stairway narrowed as it reached the top of the ziggurat, creating a theatrically effective perspective, projecting into eternity. Building, according to Giedion, was 'a sacred enterprise'. Building was the means by which man and god could be united.

When these ziggurats were built, the deities were first consulted about the selection of a site. After the necessary processes had been gone through, and the wishes of the powers ascertained, the temple was built. This is particularly important, for in Mesopotamia, layers of temple buildings have been found one over the other, as each new builder felt happy in the fact that the deity had accepted the original site. Since the temples and ziggurats were such powerful forms and

---

[1]   *The Eternal Present* Vol. II, p. 217.
[2]   *The Eternal Present* Vol. II, p. 219.

Plate 1 : Imageability. Norwich.

Plate 2 : Imageability. Dumfries.

Plate 3: Imageability. Oxford.

Plate 4: Imageability, Kensington, London.

Plate 5: *Imageability. Amsterdam, Montelbaanstoren.*

Plate 6: *Imageability. In the shadow of the Town Church,
Solbad Hall, Austria.*

Plate 7: Imageability. Jesuitenkirche, Solbad Hall.

Plate 8: Imageability. Fountain, Solbad Hall.

Plate 9: Imageability. Amsterdam, Zuiderkerkstoren.

Plate 10: Imageability. Oxford.

Plate 11: Imageability. Kensal Green Cemetery.

Plate 12: Inscape. Highgate Cemetery. (From an article by the author in the R.I.B.A. Journal of April 1968.)

Plate 13: Imageability. Salzburg, Baroque doorway.

Plate 14: Inscape. Market in the Waterlooplein, Amsterdam.

Plate 15: Imageability. Cemetery in Salzburg.

Plate 16: Imageability. Bradford-on-Avon.

Plate 17: Imageability. Salisbury.

Plate 18: Inscape. Salzburg.

Plate 19: Imageability. The Morning Star, Belfast.

dominated the town, they tended to force the succeeding layers of town into similar patterns of layout around it.

One of the most astonishing ziggurats of all was the neo-Babylonian Etemenanki, which was probably about 80 metres high. It had magnificent enrichment with strongly coloured glazed bricks and tiles. It was approached by a monumental processional way which crossed the Euphrates via a bridge and went through the Gate of Ishtar. According to Giedion, it was probably the 'longest and most ostentatious processional way' that has ever been.[1]

This excessive formalism is frequently a symbol of despotism, especially when it has no connection with its surroundings physically, and is merely 'ploughed through'. Giedion states that there is an 'uneasy sterility' when 'outward pomp' replaces 'inner intensity'.

In ancient Mesopotamia, a sacred significance was given to building which was regarded as an activity worthy of the highest levels of human imagination. The kings themselves were builders of ziggurats, for the king stood in close relationship to the gods, and there was a tradition that the king should work upon the building with his own hands.[2]

That ziggurats had a symbolic significance is beyond dispute, and their cosmic symbolism became extreme during Babylonian and Assyrian times. Etemenanki is thought to have had seven differently coloured terraces, relating to the seven planets. The idea of the ziggurat as a sacred symbol of a mountain, however, is thought to be the central one, for the sacred mountain was the middle of the world. This idea of a mountain need not only be expressed in the enormous ziggurat, for it could be suggested by a very small building of a certain form. Even an early temple platform which was little more than a podium could be regarded as a representation of a sacred mountain.[3]

The conception of centrality of the sacred mountain as being the centre of the world and the cosmos is further shown as a symbol in the relationship with the city. This is demonstrated strongly in the plan of the city of Ur (*c.* 2000 B.C.).

[1] *The Eternal Present* Vol. II, pp. 237–238.
[2] *The Eternal Present* Vol. II, p. 240.
[3] *The Art and Architecture of the Ancient Orient* pp. 6 and 7.

D

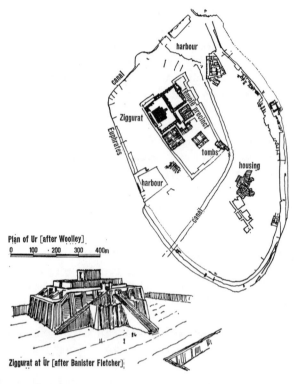

Plan of Ur [after Woolley]
0   100   200   300   400m

Ziggurat at Ur [after Banister Fletcher]

Ur [circa 2000 B.C.]   Figure No. 5

Mesopotamia was a fertile land and was well placed for trading, but it was also vulnerable to attack from the north and east. A strong military despotism developed as a result, and Babylon became not only an imperial capital, but a market centre as well. As trade developed and the power of the war-lord kings grew, secular power finally became greater than that of the priests, and the idea of the monarch as military despot superseded that of him as being near the gods. He became god-like himself. Under the Assyrian empire, the priesthood became subordinated to the power of the king, and building energies became diverted gradually to the creation of buildings to reflect the glory of the monarch. Whereas in ancient Ur, 'the temples and palaces were the only buildings with aesthetic pretensions,'[1] the palace became a dominant in later times

[1]   *The Art and Architecture of the Ancient Orient* p. 55.

until the 'small royal kiosk of Assur grows into a gigantic throne room under the Persian kings'.[1]

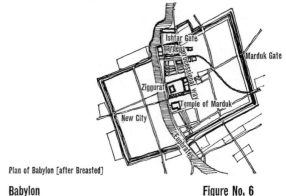

Plan of Babylon [after Breasted]

Babylon   **Figure No. 6**

The great city of Babylon had immense fortified walls within which were fields which could produce food for the population during a siege. According to Herodotus, writing about 450 B.C., the city contained the population of a nation. The city was divided by the River Euphrates which was channelled into a moat surrounding the walls. Drawbridges connected the two parts of the city, and these were raised during the night, as not only were there often threats from outside, but also the possibility of revolts within the city.[2] In the more or less rectangular plan of Babylon, the central core contained the temples and the palace. The great processional way which bisected the city was essentially a triumphal road over which the image of the god could be borne, but it would also serve to demonstrate the power and wealth of the royal household as it took part in the celebrations. Other streets cut into the main route at right angles, allowing the populace easy access to the line of the procession. Herodotus wrote of Babylon as being a city based on streets at right angles to each other, planned in relation to the wall and river. Each street ran to a gate in the main walls of the city.[3]

ANCIENT EGYPT

In ancient times towns were the seats of the ruling classes, for example, the Priest–Kings of Egypt, and the militarist–commercial

[1] *History Builds the Town* p. 21.
[2] *Ibid.* p. 22.
[3] *Towns and Town Planning* p. 2.

powers of Mesopotamia. In Ancient Egypt, power was exclusively in the hands of the Priest–King, who accumulated wealth by means of taxation, conquest, labour service by his subjects and prisoners, and by votive offerings, for he became a god-like figure himself. The Priest–Kings were a separate race as well, for they interbred, brother marrying sister. A learned ruling class under the King organized the collection of taxes and offerings, and, when the floods began, the labour service, when the peasantry went into the building industry until the land was again ready for agriculture. The ruling élite of priests, nobles and professionals was responsible to the King for the control and organization of the armies of workers necessary for large scale building operations. Sometimes this even involved building a temporary dormitory town as at Kahun (*c*. 2500 B.C.).

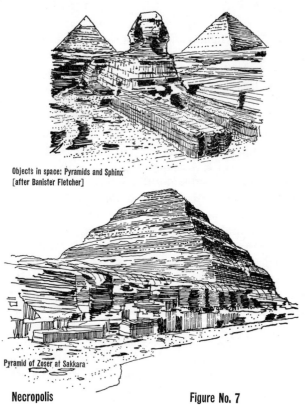

Objects in space: Pyramids and Sphinx
[after Banister Fletcher]

Pyramid of Zoser at Sakkara

Necropolis   **Figure No. 7**

The houses and palaces of Ancient Egypt were not built of durable materials, for stone was used for the architecture of power, namely, the edifices associated with the politically dominant forces: the Priest–King, nobles and Priests. They were the temples, tombs and sculptured monuments relating to the hierarchy of power, for in the then prevailing political climate, the order of belief was that the buildings associated with an after-life had to last for ever, while those in which mortal life was to be lived were, by inference, transitory, and therefore constructed of materials which would not last. The building of Necropolis was, therefore, the main object of the ruling classes, and their power was reflected in the great tombs of the Pharaohs, the Pyramids, as well as in the cities of the dead. Society was organized to produce these giant structures and complexes of houses for those no longer alive, to protect them from the elements, wild beasts and the living.

Comparing ziggurats with pyramids, we see immediately fundamental differences. Ziggurats were built within cities inhabited by living men, women and children, as staged towers upon which were temples accessible to the eyes of the many and to the priesthood in fact. The pyramids, on the other hand, were built in the desert within a city of the dead, and were inaccessible. A pyramid was both the tomb of the Pharaoh and his permanent house. It stood remote and mysterious in the sand, signifying the Pharaoh's link with the heavens. The simple mastaba was quite suddenly superseded by Zoser's pyramid (*c.* 3900 B.C.) at Sakkara which was stepped, but in a very short time the standard form was arrived at, culminating in the enormous pyramid of Cheops. Pyramid building spanned a few centuries, whereas ziggurats were the foci of religious cults throughout Mesopotamian history. Yet pyramid and ziggurat have two things in common: they derive from a seeking of vertical man-made mountains as a symbol of contact between earth, man, sky and deity; and they are both formed on squares as an underlying basic pattern.

We must not forget that the Ancient Egyptian world was full of symbols: where now and then, life and after-life, sacred and profane, were united and formed an entity. The architecture of Ancient Egypt, unchanging, stylized and monumental, expressed what Giedion calls 'a world of the eternal present – the unending continuance of existence'.[1] Giedion also reminds us that Schiaparelli,

[1] *The Eternal Present* Vol. II, p. 342.

writing in 1884, drew our attention to the existence of pyramids in
a symbolic frame of relationships, so that they are not separate
tombs, but are seen together as cult objects in a group.
Yet each pyramid has many significant aspects to be considered.
Zoser's pyramid could be a symbol of a ladder or stairway to the
heavens, unlike the ziggurat, where the steps led to a temple and
were not superhumanly large, and the idea of contact with the
deity was altogether more complex. Classic pyramids have other
symbolism. The triangular motif is a symbol of both vulva and
phallus, mountain, fire, water, rays of the sun, but the superimposi-
tion on the base which is a square is even more significant. Four was
a sacred number to the Egyptians, and was related to the four winds,
the four directions of heaven, the four faces of the gods, the four
parts of Egypt, the four columns on which the sky rested, and the
four jars for the internal organs of embalmed bodies.[1] The square
is an expression of the sacred number, and the orientation of the
pyramids to the cardinal points of the compass stresses the symbolism of the relation between the pyramids and the cosmos.

The sanctity and remoteness, in their different ways, of ziggurat,
temple and pyramid were responsible for a fact common to ancient
cultures, namely that because the people could see these edifices,
walk round them, but never enter them, architectural forms tended
to be enormous bulks in space to accentuate their significance.

MINOS AND MYCENAE

Minoan civilization seems to have developed in Crete from around
2000 B.C. Trade and piracy seem to have produced much of the
wealth which tended to be concentrated in the hands of the Priest–
King. Knossos emerged as the centre of a state by 1500 B.C., and
excavations have demonstrated that manufactured goods and huge
warehousing enterprises were the backbone of the economy rather
than an agrarian one.

The palace of Knossos was in turn the centre of a town which was
the heart of a trading empire, the existence of which depended on
naval power. This naval power was such that the King of Crete was
able to establish fortified strong-points in Greece, which is not easy
to invade overland. It is significant that Knossos was not fortified,[2]
but the colonies founded at Troy, Thebes, Argos, Orchomenos,

---

[1]   *The Eternal Present* Vol. II, p. 348.
[2]   *The Greek Experience* p. 7.

Tiryns and Mycenae were strongholds, and they, together with Knossos, formed collectively what we know as Minoa. However, these colonies were small and of predominantly military character, the architectural dominants being the huge fortified walls and the stronghold of the rulers.

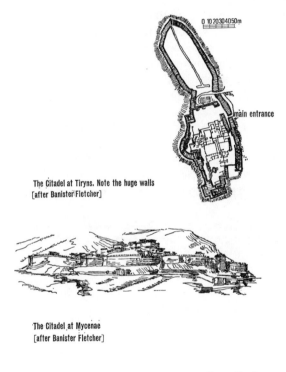

The Citadel at Tiryns. Note the huge walls
[after Banister Fletcher]

The Citadel at Mycenae
[after Banister Fletcher]

Walls as dominants   **Figure No. 8**

After the destruction of Knossos in 1450 B.C., Mycenae became the centre of an empire dedicated to military and naval conquest, piracy and plunder. This empire, although continuing some of the older traditions of Minoan trade, became highly organized as a fighting machine under the monarchs or war-lords of Mycenae.

After 1200 B.C., a related people, the Dorians, destroyed the military power of Mycenae, which had probably become over-expanded as well as indulging in inter-city squabbling. The Dorians undoubtedly were a sea-power, otherwise Mycenae could not have been so effectively and quickly beaten.

Certainly after the Dorian conquest a dark age descended. The architecture and planning of Minoan and Mycenean cultures herald the Hellenic, but there was undoubtedly a lapse in the continuity of development.[1]

Minoan cities had centres comprising palace and an open area for social activities, whereas those of Mycenae were overshadowed by military strong-points, so that the towns were mainly 'stuck on' to the citadels. Thus Minoan and Hellenic cities share a common central open space, where social activities could be carried on, while Mycenean cities had enormous 'cyclopean' walls and emphasized the politically dominant militarism of the rulers.[2]

Apart from excavations which have told us something of these early cultures, legend has handed down to us stories of the Minotaur and the labyrinth. The concept of a labyrinth is a very old one and may be a mandala form. It is possible that the Greek Key pattern we know from classical decoration was in fact a stylized symbol of this labyrinth which, in its day, may have been the central symbol of Minoan concepts of man's relation to the Cosmos.

---

[1] Recent theories have suggested this lapse was due to a great natural disaster, probably an earthquake, tidal waves and volcanic activity.
[2] See also *How the Greeks Built Cities* pp. 2 and 3.

III

The Bedrock of European Culture

THE GREEKS

Introduction

Peoples from the Danube valley, it seems, were the ones who destroyed the Aegean cultures previously mentioned.[1] These tribally organized invaders were nomadic and had iron weapons. They were the barbarian Greeks who conquered the eastern Mediterranean, while the Carthaginians developed their culture in the western parts of the coast.

In early times, before the tribes took to military conquest, they were probably matriarchal in character, the women mating freely with the men of their fancy. Sons did not know who their fathers were, and it was the desire to hand down property through the male line, together with the discovery that warfare could be profitable for the loot, that gave males the dominant role in society, led to monogamy and the decline in the status of women in Greek society.

After 2000 B.C., Boetia, Attica and the Peloponnese were conquered by Ionic tribes. As the millennium progressed, so did the organization of the nomadic peoples, so that they were able to build fleets strong enough to challenge the sea power of the Aegean cultures. Knossos fell in 1450 B.C., and the Dorians held the lion's share, while Ionians and Aeolians settled in Asia Minor. The tribes were cut off from each other as they became less nomadic and settled down, for natural boundaries separated them. Their economies were based on agriculture, mainly livestock farming, but olives and vines added to the output and encouraged trade with the lands round the Black Sea where corn was produced. The topography and the economy, however, were such that there was no reason for large centralized warehousing or a central state.

With the growth of trade and the possibilities of outside threat, this state of affairs altered, for communities tended to league

---

[1] A recent theory is that of the natural disaster mentioned in a footnote on p. 22.

together for commerce, defence, religious celebration, and, ultimately, for common government. From 2000 B.C. to the beginning of the first millennium, political organization was rudimentary, and it was not until groups of settlements coagulated, forming nuclei in each area that we see the beginnings of the *polis* or city-state.

Religion played an important part in the origins of the ancient city, and often the gods were consulted to determine sites.[1] Religion was an essential part of life and ritual, and not a separate entity. Different gods were greater obstacles than natural frontiers in the formation of states. Religion has, in all ages, been a dominant force in the selection of sites for towns or cities. Hills, springs, sites of visions or places of burial of politico-religious figures have all been significant factors in city-founding, and it must be remembered that hills and springs had symbolic and magical qualities as well as obvious material virtues. The Delphic Oracle was consulted on matters of city siting, and it was said that Apollo himself ordained that Delphi should stand where it was built.[2]

Natural features such as the acropolis in the Attic plain were obvious choices for the siting and protection of the temples of gods worshipped by the ethnic group.[3] Such a place was also, obviously, a place of refuge in the event of attack. In the beginning of development of the city-state, the acropolis might in fact *be* the polis. It was the dominant, the fortress, sanctuary and seat of the monarch, when the Greeks had kings. The dwellings were grouped round the base of the strongpoint, usually on the south side, but as the town expanded the houses embraced the acropolis.

The design of the Greek city and its architectural elements were directly the result of the political climate: 'They followed at every step the cultural, religious and political evolution of the Greeks.'[4]

The centre of the lower town was the agora, where the people met for political, commercial or social reasons. Agora and acropolis formed the two nuclei of the polis, both catering for Biosphere and Noösphere in different ways. As time went by and political changes took place, the relationship between acropolis and agora changed too, the agora gaining in importance as the acropolis waned in significance, until finally it became the heart of the polis. Wycherley states that as the government changed from a monarchy to a demo-

[1] *The West European City* pp. 254–255.
[2] *Greek Civilization* p. 141.
[3] *A Prospect of Cities* p. 5.
[4] *How the Greeks Built Cities* p. 4.

cracy, the acropolis became an appendage, although it probably gained in sanctity and could still, of course, serve as a fortress.[1]

As a more sophisticated society developed so did institutions, including those among which the political power, which had once been the monarch's alone, was divided. As these grew, so an architecture developed to house each function, but this was a slow process.

When political functions developed and commerce expanded, so the temples of the gods became more enriched. In early times the temples were the only buildings with aesthetic pretensions, and as the polis became more powerful and wealthy, so its gods were honoured with richer and more elaborate temples.

Athens in the fifth century B.C. [after various sources]

Athens   **Figure No. 9**

The two nuclei, agora and acropolis, had dwellings grouped round them, and beyond them, in turn, was a wall, so that a fortified town resulted with the acropolis as the citadel. The town became in its turn the nucleus of the polis, which included both the town, its umland and hinterland. The polis is therefore *town* and *country*.

The agora, heart of the daily political, social and commercial functions of the polis, had streets radiating from it, leading up to the gates of the city. The overall plan, however, was not ordered in

[1] *How the Greeks Built Cities* p. 7.

any noticeably geometric way; that developed in later times. Round the agora, the public buildings such as the bouleuterion, stoa and fountain houses were grouped informally, together with temples and shrines. Gymnasium, stadium and theatre were usually placed where the topography was favourable. The wall was not a corset into which the city was forced. Instead, it was built after the town had found its shape, and enclosing walls were not normal until the fifth century B.C. Prior to this time, the acropolis had been the fortress to which the polis turned.[1]

The Greek city derived its quality from elements peculiar to Hellenic culture. Undoubtedly the most important of these elements was the agora, which ousted the acropolis from its central position in life by the fifth century. Yet the reverence in which the acropolis was held is important too, for, although the acropolis was, in a sense, an archaic survival, it symbolized the spirit of Hellenic creativity, since so much had been lavished on its temples and monuments. It was also The Past, looked on as a visible reality. The Greeks knew of the calendars of Babylon and Egypt, but never attempted to make them form part of life. Even Thucydides considered that little of any note had occurred before his own day (*c.* 400 B.C.) apart from the achievements of Periclean Athens. We see, therefore, that the Past as Present was acceptable in visual form and was treasured, but otherwise had little to commend it to the Greek mind.

The early city-states tended to be situated a short distance from the coast for fear of attack from the sea, as piracy, so Thucydides informs us, was rampant at one time. Piraeus was connected with Athens by a long fortified wall; and acted as the port of Athens.

Greek colonial development in Hellenic times was undertaken in a different spirit from that of the time of Alexander. There seems to have been little desire for conquest or military glory. When the parent state became crowded, colonists left to seek a suitable site, and, by trading and bringing sufficient skills with them, they ensured a viable economic existence. Perhaps the most interesting aspect of the 'colonies' was their political independence. This is true also of the parent states of Greece which were independent of each other. Practically the whole of the eastern shores of the Mediterranean became settled by independent city-states, all owing their origins to the great Hellenic mother-culture. These city-states were

[1]   *How the Greeks Built Cities* p. 10.

linked by the sea and by trade. Sites were usually promontories which would ensure escape by sea and easy defence by land at minimum cost.[1]

With regard to defence, the fortified walls were the last but one line of defence. Battles were fought in the open, and the army only withdrew to the walls if it was in trouble. The acropolis could be the citadel, as once it had been the only defence. In the days when the acropolis had been the seat of a ruling class it could be a protection against the citizens as well as for them. When Hellenic democracy developed, the populace became the protected, and so walls were built round their houses. An acropolis under armed occupation was thought of as a symbol of tyranny.[2] The walls were, on the other hand, symbols of autonomy.

If the agora was all life, argument, business and pleasure, the acropolis acquired, during the fifth century, a serenity, where the gods lived on in their fine temples, for art and religion were inextricably connected. A city could be a city minus a wall, but for the Greeks it could not be such without an agora, gymnasium, theatre or stadium. 'As for walls,' said Plato,[3] 'I would leave them to slumber peacefully in the earth . . . A wall . . . commonly breeds a certain softness of soul in the townsmen.' Plato advised that the whole town should form one unbroken wall if it really were needed. The wall, according to Wycherley, 'was not normally a dominant factor in the plan . . .'[4]

The growing dominance of the agora in Greek town plans encouraged enrichment of the buildings associated with it. Municipal buildings tended to group round it, and the stoa, an open colonnade, became a characteristic feature of the agora. Cults of gods and goddesses encouraged the erection of temples, altars and statuary in or near the agora. The gods, as it were, stepped down from the heights and mixed with the people in the new democratic Hellenic life. As trade developed, so bankers, merchants, exporters and shipping agents moved in on the agora and founded their business premises near it. The stoa was not only used for markets, but for exchanges, surgeries, and a place for argument, drinking and social intercourse. The agora became the heart of the polis, and the agora of Athens became the heart of Attica.

[1] *A Prospect of Cities* pp. 5 and 6.
[2] *How the Greeks Built Cities* p. 37.
[3] *The Laws* pp. 161–162.
[4] *How the Greeks Built Cities* p. 39.

Athens had an enormous agora, and is famed in literature. Law was administered from offices near it, and politics was involved in its daily affairs. The Heliaea court had its place in the agora, and even in earliest times, law had been administered from it. Civic, religious, commercial, judicial, political and social functions combined in the agora to give it its unique architectural expressions.

Shrines and temples were important edifices in the polis, and apart from the temples on the acropolis, there would be others associated with the agora. Priests could be accommodated in the stoa, and scattered shrines and images could always be in view of the people. Undoubtedly the greatest centre of religion in Greece was at Olympia, which acted as the Rome of Hellenic religious life. Associated with such a centre were the gymnasia, stadium and treasuries.

Yet it was not at Olympia that we find the finest expressions of Greek civilization, but in Athens. Threatened by Persia, the Hellenic world formed a league to combat the menace, and Athens succeeded Sparta as the leader. Treasuries emptied their contents into Athens as contributions towards the war effort, but these became tributes to Athens as well. Power corrupts, and Athens became a new tyrant, head of an empire of formerly free city-states. Pericles, who was general of Athens from 443 B.C. to 430 B.C., justified Athenian imperialism in the name of democracy. He regarded Athens as the home of Greek learning, and so set out to Athenianize all other city-states. These imperial ambitions were to be celebrated in a demonstration of all that Athens could do in sculpture and architecture: the new buildings of the Athenian acropolis. The Parthenon and all the other significant and beautiful buildings were erected with funds raised by levying tributes from the other city-states. Athene was a goddess of war and her statue became the symbol of the glory of Athens in terms of military and artistic prowess as well as of wealth and political power. The Goddess of Athens became for a time the Pan-Hellenic goddess. The Parthenon honoured a goddess, but it also honoured Athens. The proportions and detailing of the temples were remarkable, and not least of the achievements of Greek sculpture were lavished on the pediments of this extraordinary building. Athene emerges triumphant in her battle, and prevails, symbolizing the triumph of the Athenians themselves. As the Greek gods were anthropomorphous, so they were sculpted, and their interventions in human affairs were pictorially represented.

We see the ruins on the acropolis today in a rosy light. To us they are the epitome of a wonderful culture, but we see them now, broken, washed and weathered, forgetting that when they were new they were painted polychromatically, in hard, bright primary colours. There is something else wrong too, for in the years of Pericles, it was decreed that the expounding of astronomical theory was a criminal offence, and we know that the Greeks knew of the existence of the arch, yet a traditional method and form of building was used to replace those ruined by the Persians. There is something curiously reactionary about the Athenian masterpieces, for all that there is to admire in them. Further investigation (and we need not investigate very far) reveals that the entire Greek system was built upon slavery. With all the talk of democracy, freedom and reason, we might not expect this, but it is an undeniable fact. C. M. Bowra, in an article in *Cities of Destiny*[1] states that the defect might not be so great as we might suppose, because Athens differed from many slave owning societies in that it had a 'large proportion' of free men to slaves. This proportion, we are told, 'has been calculated' as being 'two to one.' Now this proportion might seem to be an enormous one, and added to slaves as such were women, who might be regarded as little more than slaves. Yet, at the same time, we must not forget that 'slaves' in the context of the Greek city-state means something rather different from the term as we understand it today. Korn states that the population of the Athenian polis was about 300,000, of whom 115,000 were slaves. Engels estimated that the number of slaves was 365,000 while free citizens numbered 135,000.[2] A married woman in ancient Greece had few rights: the best-off were priestesses and high-class courtesans. It may well be that because of the very existence of slavery, the Greeks felt no need to pursue scientific discoveries and put them to use, hence their indifference to the arch and the Periclean antagonism to astronomy. Since society could rest upon an enormous labour force of slaves, the same incentive to develop scientifically and economically just was not there. If slavery had been challenged, the whole character of the polis would have changed.[3] It was logical, therefore, having accepted it, to rationalize slavery and explain away any guilt by arguing its necessity. The love of reason, therefore, seems spurious,

---

[1] *Cities of Destiny* pp. 43–44.
[2] *History Builds the Town* p. 27.
[3] *The Condition of Man* p. 24.

in a way, for it does not seem to have proceeded far into the very nature of Greek life. The individual self, so admired, was existing in the polis, which was, in a sense, its symbol, but the polis also contained the quarters of the slaves. The individual self, therefore, was only possible in the leisured class of free *men*. 'Men' is deliberately emphasized since women were not treated as individual selves either. A leisured body of men who had time for polite society and pleasurable and civilized pursuits, was in fact carried on the backs of the members of the slave class, in which could be included the women. The Athens of Pericles was vanquished by the feelings aroused over the policies which had contributed to its visual glory. Repression, not co-operation with other city-states, was the means Athens used in order to bring all Greece within the Athenian influence.

To the Greeks, reason was a more logical foundation for life than the senses. Geometry and rules could guide the builders much better than the eye, so ideal proportions and techniques were arrived at. Although the sciences were not developed, they were to a certain extent used, in that theories of geometry were applied to the development and refining of a *purely traditional form of building*. The Parthenon is the logical outcome of reason applied to traditional forms. Seen today it appears marvellously evocative and incredibly beautiful, yet, seen in imagination, as it was, its beauty is terrifying: hard, precise, glittering, polychromatic, cold and immensely proud.

Reason depends on the continuity and development of a civilization which it orders, but Reason must go on reasoning, until it may destroy qualities in a culture. If one tries to analyse what cannot be analysed, or compartment what cannot be compartmented, one deceives oneself by tending to ignore qualities which defy classification. Reason could reason the inhabitants of Olympus out of existence, but new gods came to redress the balance, yet only accentuated the split in the culture. Apollo and Dionysus were opposed and differing symbols of the difficulties Greek culture faced. If Apollo represents reason, order, measure and light, Dionysus is the incarnation of unreason, liberation, anaesthesia of guilt, and release of the inhibitions imposed by order. It is significant that the rise of the cult of Dionysus coincides with the development of *Hellenistic* culture, with its new geometric order in city plans. Dionysus was honoured in the vineyard and the forest, far away from the city and its civilized order. Bacchic rites and pastoral imagery represented

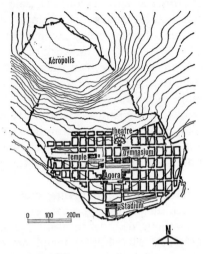

Plan of Priene [after various sources]

Priene   Figure No. 10

an opposite pole to that of the city and its institutions, reason, order and geometrically beautiful buildings.

Thus life became elevated and reason became obscured, whereas if Dionysus and Apollo had been reconciled, a new and incredibly rich culture could well have emerged. It was Nietzsche who, in his *Birth of Tragedy*, showed us that the failure to accept the wholeness of life was the basic problem of our own civilization in Western Europe. He saw that order is usually order at the expense of life, and that ecstasy and joy are crushed by Order which sees them as threats. If Apollo and Dionysus could be united, a profound harmony in a culture could result, and Nietzsche held up the example of Greece to us as a lesson for our own age, despite its obvious differences.

Plato

An examination of the antique town cannot rely on excavation alone. The accounts from classical writers yield the keys of our knowledge, for the philosophers discussed the city-states and left us records, whereas so little remains for the archaeologist to discover.

Plato (b. 428 B.C., d. 347 B.C.), considering a new foundation of

E

a city, stated that proper attention would be paid to the subject of architecture in all its details, including the temples and walls. It was a subject which came before marriage, which would be regarded as the 'crown and completion' of the work of building a city. He thought that the temples should be grouped round the market place, and scattered throughout the city on elevated sites. Here he obviously had an image of the acropolis of old. Nearby should be the courts and offices of the magistrates. Regularity of planning was considered essential, and an Urban Commission was to be set up charged with the task of 'prohibiting all interference with the plan of the city by buildings or excavations on the part of private persons'.[1]

Plato considered that neither city nor constitution nor man would be perfect until the philosophers took charge of the city, and found it obedient to them, or until the ruling classes developed a 'true love of philosophy'.[2] The philosopher-planner was charged by Plato with the task of realizing 'in individual and city his heavenly vision'.[3] Plato asked if people would be incredulous if it were said that a city would 'never know happiness until its draughtsmen are artists who have as their pattern the divine'.

In *The Republic*, Plato tried to fuse the best qualities of Spartan and Athenian culture in his Utopian State which, he thought, could produce a cultured, reliable and courageous people. He did not doubt that the city was the only unit suitable for the development of the society he so desired. Union between states was only desirable when threatened from outside, thus through the independence of small city-states, democracy was possible because each free citizen could take a direct part in his government. Such a state of affairs would have been impossible in a larger unit. Slavery was essential to the Platonic Utopia, for, as Aristotle points out, the citizens could not have had any leisure necessary for active participation in public affairs if slavery had not existed.

Plato insisted that there would be an ideal number of citizens, and that it would be assumed that five thousand and forty landowners would occupy the same number of holdings. Practically, this number could be divided up for various functions, and it was arrived at by multiplying the numbers one to seven successively. It

---

[1]   *The Laws* VI, 778, 779. pp. 161 and 162.
[2]   *The Republic* VI, 499. p. 192.
[3]   *Ibid.* 500. p. 193.

is thus divisible by the numbers one to ten and by twelve.[1] Yet this concern with numbers was not merely practical, but had its origins in traditions of magic and cosmological belief, and was used to express concepts of order.[2]

Plato considered the ideal city in detail in *The Laws*. First of all, it was to be built inland, approximately ten miles from the coast where there would be harbours. No other city was to be anywhere near: this was to be 'The very reason for the settlement'. A 'rugged rather than level' site was to be selected, and the surrounding area would provide sufficient for necessities and a little trade. Too fertile an area would encourage settlers who would upset the balance of population, and a coastal situation would encourage 'much refined vice' as well as developing 'wholesale traffic and retail huckstering'.[3]

Two centuries before Plato, Pythagoras founded a government at Croton which raised the city to a position of considerable importance in Calabria. Thus we see it as not being a totally Utopian idea for a philosopher to found a city, and much in Plato's Republic could have been accomplished within the context of the dialogues of his day. The idealism of Pythagoras and his denunciations of worldly pleasures produced the unusual spectacle of the wealthy of Croton giving all their treasures to the statue of Hera. The joys of renunciation have always given polite society an exquisite pleasure, and the liberation of the ladies in that they were encouraged to participate in rites of public worship added a novelty. Now it is curious that the two chief theoretical doctrines of Pythagoras were those of metempsychosis and the reduction of everything to a system of numbers, while the practical doctrine, namely that mankind was to be organized like a community of eastern monks, suggested the dissolution of a rational urban life. A curious survival of the Pythagoran number-system is reported by Norman Douglas in *Old Calabria*.[4] Apparently some Graeco-Roman traditions still lived on when Douglas was writing (1911-13), one of which was the habit of spitting three times in the presence of a child being suckled, and then shouting, also three times, 'Otto-Nove'. For all his reputation, the sage of Croton has much to answer for. There is a lesson to be learnt from the fate of Sybaris, a city near Croton, whose name was

---

[1] *A Prospect of Cities* p. 11, and *The Laws* V, 738. p. 120.
[2] *The Ideal City* p. 13.
[3] *The Laws* IV, 704 and 705. pp. 87 and 88.
[4] p. 322.

synonymous with luxury, gorgeously clad inhabitants, splendid cuisine and a generally rarefied aestheticism. In 510 B.C. the Sybarites provoked the citizens of Croton into war, which the latter won easily, possibly due to the fact that the Sybarite cavalry could not function properly since the horses were taught to dance to the sound of the flute.[1] Not satisfied with what was undoubtedly a just victory, however, the Pythagoreans destroyed Sybaris by flooding, an act of barbarism which contributed to the end of Hellenic civilization in Italy.

Seen in perspective, Sybaris must have been the epitome of style. Its colony at Paestum, of which remains still exist, is a testament of the dignity of its architecture.

Plato's splendid yearnings as revealed in *The Republic* are full of idealism, and a belief in perfection as he saw it. *The Laws*, a much later work, is more sober in its arguments, for Plato had failed to regenerate Syracuse, while Pythagoras had succeeded in regenerating Croton. Plato in a sense is a symbol of old Athens, and he was in a way a survival of it at the end of the Peloponnesian War. Athens had been ruined by fighting, her own greed and tyranny, and ravished by the great plague which reduced her population alarmingly. The struggle of Plato can be seen as an attempt to restore order and reason to a culture which was falling apart. His Utopian Republic is a vision of order in approaching chaos, and if at times it seems to lean too much to the mystical, we must realize that Plato saw the dangers of banishing the gods to some windy limbo where they no longer had any significance. A curious feature of Plato's Utopia, however, is that he advised the subordination of the arts, and even the abandoning of some of them. The reason for his declarations on this topic was that in the political climate of his own day he saw that the teachers were producing clever orators, specialists in rhetoric and airy aesthetes, and not the good all rounders that Athens needed in her period of reconstruction. Plato in a sense lowered his sights in a vain attempt to save his own civilization. Attacked by many, and not entirely without cause, he possessed qualities of wisdom, courage, a sense of justice, and a temperate view of things. His Republic was to be ruled by philosophers who possessed the wisdom; guarded by men of courage; justice was to pervade its institutions, and finally temperance was to be a virtue of all. Significantly, Plato, although he needed slaves, sought to free

---

[1] *The Greek Experience* p. 98.

women from their slave-like position in society. He took the example of Sparta, suggesting that women should be given equality with men, and that the excessive domesticity of family life should become less constricting in that women should join the men for public eating and drinking and take part in the social life of the city to an extent they hitherto had not been able to do.

Plato failed to realize, however, that cities are social phenomena and are in a constant state of change, therefore his ordered society could not develop, and the *status quo* would have to be rigidly enforced if his ideas were to survive. The perfect constitution and physical structure of his city would be rigidly protected by guardians of civic beauty and public morals. A complete censorship was to be in operation, and geometrical precision was to be used in building.

That life should be arrested, and perfection reached, protected, and forced to remain static, was a central conviction of the Greek mind, for the community, the polis, was a work of art.[1] The means Plato sought to protect his vision seem to us to be totalitarian, especially such unsavoury methods as the 'organized sneaking' Cecil Stewart mentions.[2]

Aristotle and Hippodamus

Aristotle (b. 384 B.C., d. 322 B.C.) was critical of the Platonic approach on many counts, especially in that he felt the political structure of a permanent ruling class would cause discontent in many sectors of society. 'You may be sure,' Aristotle asserts, 'that if the methods advocated in Plato's *Republic* were sound, they would not have gone unrecognized.'[3]

Aristotle states that the polis is a creation of nature and that man is a political animal, and if he cannot live in a society, then he is no part of the polis. The city, broadly speaking, consisted for Aristotle of a group of persons large enough to be self-sufficient. It was an 'association of families and villages in a perfect and self-sufficing existence,'[4] dwelling in a single place and building a 'good life'.

Specifically, Aristotle, in his treatise on town planning as such, suggests that the city should be accessible from land and sea, and also within reach of the countryside associated with it. Ideally, the

[1] *The Condition of Man* p. 30.
[2] In *A Prospect of Cities* p. 12.
[3] *Politics* II, 1264a, p. 36.
[4] *Politics* III, 1281a, p. 82.

site should be by the sea, mainly for commercial and defence reasons.[1] Health is an important consideration, and Aristotle suggests that the city should face the east and be sheltered from the north wind.[2] Political and administrative requirements as well as strategic ones came under his scrutiny, the most desirable topography being such that an enemy would find the city impregnable, yet the citizens would have easy egress. Good water supply was essential, and he draws our attention to the necessity of separating drinking water from water 'destined for other purposes'.

Aristotle made some interesting remarks on the symbolism of the acropolis. Defences, he declared, will vary with different constitutions. 'An acropolis is suited to an oligarchy or a monarchy, but a level site to a democracy.'[3] Neither suited an aristocracy, which was better off in a number of strongpoints. It is at this point (*Politics* VII, 1330b) that Aristotle mentions Hippodamus in connection with the layout of houses, which he considered 'more pleasant and generally more convenient' if the 'modern and regular lay-out introduced by Hippodamus' was followed. Yet Aristotle suggested that in order to confuse an enemy, irregular traditional layouts should be included in the city combined with a geometric approach. He considered beauty to be an important quality of the city. Sensibly, he discarded Plato's views on walls, fully realizing that the enemy might be superior to the defence, so walls were necessary, not only to protect the citizens, but the town, since siege weapons in his day were improving technically.

Hippodamus of Miletus, regarded as the first town planner, though there were undoubtedly many before him, is famous through his appearance in *Politics*. He had flowing hair, wore warm but cheap clothing and expensive ornaments, and cultivated 'eccentric habits'. He aspired to 'learning in the field of natural science,' and he was interested in finding out what was the best form of government.

The city which Hippodamus designed was to have a population of 10,000, divided into three classes – artisans, farmers and a professional army.[4] Aristotle considered this last innovation to be a highly dangerous idea, since the professional military men would indubitably grasp political power for themselves. Land, in the

---

[1]　*Politics* VII, 1327b, pp. 200–201.
[2]　*Ibid.* 1330a, p. 206.
[3]　*Ibid.* 1330b, p. 206.
[4]　*Politics* II, 1267b, p. 46.

Miletus   Figure No. 11

Hippodamian scheme of things, was to be divided into three parts for sacred, public and private purposes. He suggested major reforms of the legal system; that people who benefited the state should be rewarded; that dependants of men killed in action should be supported by the state; and that magistrates were to be elected and charged with watching over the interests of the public, of aliens and of orphans.

Aristotle tells us that Hippodamus was responsible for the design of Piraeus, of which we know very little save that it was a basic gridiron plan. He may have carried out some work in Calabria, and Strabo says he planned Rhodes, but Wycherley says this is unlikely.[1]

The gridiron, if laid on a varied series of contours, can produce interesting stepped streets, vistas and terraces. Hippodamian technique took all the elements of the polis: agora, temples, theatre, gymnasium and stadium, and fitted them into a rectangular pattern, yet the walls respected the lie of the land and had little relation to the gridiron within.

[1] *How the Greeks Built Cities* p. 17.

Priene, a colonial town of the fourth century, is a good example of Hippodamian method. An Ionian city, on the coast of Asia Minor, with a population of around 4000, it had everything which constituted the polis, very ingeniously arranged within a gridiron. It was built on the southern side of an 1100 foot high mountain, and the east-west streets followed the level contour lines while the north-south ones cut across them and so were stepped and ramped. The agora was physically the centre of the town as well as spiritually, and the acropolis was relegated to the bleak mountain-top, un-adorned with temples or monuments. A wall loosely enclosed the whole, including the mountain top.

Alexander the Great

Aristotle remains supremely important in any discussion of Greek town planning, not only because of his references to Hippodamus and his own views, but because he was the mentor of Alexander the Great. The latter may be credited with the foundations of many cities stretching along the lines of communication from Macedonia to Afghanistan. The sites must have been chosen with amazing sureness of touch, for many cities have disappeared beneath new cities of later cultures, among which may be named the Egyptian Alexandria, Kabul and Samarkand. These foundations, unlike the Hellenic colonies, were built for strategic reasons: they were part of a Grand Plan of imperial conquest. Garrisoned, they would act as bases for the armies and as centres for the cultivation and gathering of food for the army.

Alexander attempted to unify various races under his rule, and the growth of the eastern cities and their subsequent enrichment as pearls in the imperial crown gave rise to a new culture which we know as Hellenistic. Cities of this period have the Hippodamian approach, and the Egyptian Alexandria displayed a plan that was almost rectangular itself.

Alexandria would possibly not have succeeded as a city had not Alexander died a premature death. Since he had been attempting to carry the focus of Hellenistic civilization eastwards, his sudden demise and his merging with myth removed the impetus of imperial ambition. The forces, therefore, of Hellenistic culture swung west again, so that the Aegean and eastern Mediterranean became once more the centre of the Greek world. Alexandria was founded in 332 B.C., and a great future was predicted for it. The building of the city on the seashore is a result of the safe political climate of a world free from raiders. It is also a reminder that the advice of Aristotle was being followed rather than that of Plato.

The architectural dominants of Alexandria were Pharos – the great lighthouse – the theatre, palaces and Gate of the Sun (a triumphal arch). It is significant that the main east–west street, Canopus Street, was a three-mile-long processional way, complete with arch of triumph. The agora is relegated to an insignificant position in the plan. Pharos was crowned with a status of Ptolemy I, one of Alexander's generals, who became king of Alexandria in 323 B.C. and founded a dynasty which ended with the death of Cleopatra in 30 B.C.

Alexandria   Figure No. 12

Like other Hellenistic cities, Alexandria associated itself with Tyche, goddess of Fortune, who personified the traditions of the city state,[1] yet the Hellenic traditions were rapidly going by the board. The new age spread the culture of Greece far over the then known world, but lost its centre or nucleus, for the old gods had disappeared almost entirely into obscurity, and neither Olympus nor Athens could be the centre of a culture which had become cosmopolitan and had its centre of gravity somewhere farther east.

[1] *The Ideal City* p. 14.

Superstitions grew, and the new Hellenistic monarchs took on the titles of the gods themselves. Even Alexander had proclaimed himself son of Zeus-Ammon and therefore heir to the pharaohs. Greece had overstretched itself.

We have seen that Greek consciousness seemed to lack a sense of time in history, for the Odyssey is a mixture of historical fact and myth. There was also the attitude of Thucydides mentioned earlier in this chapter. The merging of the colossus of Alexander with the god Dionysus demonstrated that Alexander was, for his successors, uninteresting as a political figure, but in his kinship with a god his mythological significance is of absorbing importance. Had Alexander the Great been of more abstemious habits and had he been identified with a less inebriating deity, such as Apollo, there is room for speculation as to the outcome of history.

Alexander had set Rome the example of imperial conquest while weakening Greek city-states in the west by the attractions of migration, so that within a very short time Greece was to collapse in the face of Roman conquest.

In Hellenistic times the growth of the autocracies was echoed and symbolized in the plans of the cities. Pergamon is an outstanding

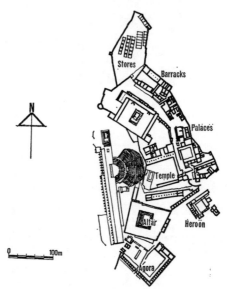

Pergamon: the upper city   Figure No. 13

example of the Hellenistic approach. The upper town, consisting of theatre, agora (in a minor position), palaces, barracks, great altar, temples, stoa and library was separated from the lower town by a fortified wall. The upper town was magnificent, extravagant and overbearing. The great altar itself is an astonishingly monumental work. The political power of the king was symbolized in the upper town which was in reality looking down on where the ordinary people lived.

The lack of interest in new techniques of building and the defence of the Greek vision of the world recalls to mind the way in which the Church defended the central position of the earth theory against the views of Copernicus. Yet the mediaeval cathedrals aspired ever upwards to the heavens, while Greek temples were static and earthbound. The Doric temple, in its apotheosis, the Parthenon, seems to be symbolic of the Greek creative spirit. It is perfection carried to a rarefied degree, but, like Plato's Utopia, is static in its perfection.

Jacob Burckhardt once said that the expressions on the faces of the Greek gods and goddesses were full of a terrible melancholy. He suggested that it was surprising that the Olympians should be sad, living as they did, possessing everything, but yet they lived for only themselves and inflicted suffering on all the world, and so they had to perish.

Rilke says somewhere that beauty is the beginning of terror, and that every angel is terrible. Perhaps he saw in the angelic orders and their perfection the same terror that the present writer sees in the Parthenon. Nietzsche thought that the despair of the Greeks was reconciled to life through the perfection of beauty. Both Burckhardt and Nietzsche realized that Attic tragedy was real in that a kind of resigned pessimism pervaded their culture.

Periclean Athens, using the words of W. B. Yeats, gave birth to a 'terrible beauty' symbolized in the perfection of the Parthenon.[1]

THE JEWS

The Jewish tradition is important in this study, for Biblical subject matter and imagery were potent forces in the development of European ideals.

The architectural and religious dominance of the Temple and the politico-religious importance of Jerusalem developed the former

[1] *Easter 1916.*

as a symbol of the latter. Jerusalem is represented in a synagogue in Dura-Europos as a Hellenistic building[1] with a porch. Dr. Rosenau states that the Temple represented the idea of redemption and fulfilment. It was therefore associated with the concept of Jerusalem as a celestial city.

Significantly, the court of the temple was an exact square,[2] and the room for the Ark of the Covenant was 'twenty cubits in length, and twenty cubits in breadth, and twenty cubits in the height thereof: and he (Solomon) overlaid it with pure gold; and *so* covered the altar *which was of* cedar'.[3] Thus the sanctuary was a cube, and the cubic form was an ancient mandala symbol. The square is, as we have seen previously, found in ancient symbolism. The sanctuary and courtyard grow to the city itself in the apocalyptic vision of St. John the Divine:

'And the city lieth foursquare, and the length is as large as the breadth: and he measured the city with the reed, twelve thousand furlongs. The length and the breadth and the height of it are equal.' The city wall had twelve foundations of precious stones of different colours, an idea we have already encountered in Babylon, and it had twelve gates. 'And I saw no temple therein: for the Lord God Almighty and the Lamb are the temple of it.'[4] The heavenly city, new Jerusalem, is described in curious terms by St. John, for he says: 'And I John saw the holy city, new Jerusalem, coming down from God out of heaven, prepared as a bride adorned for her husband.'[5]

The magical number twelve, together with the twelve colours of the precious stones: jasper, sapphire, chalcedony, emerald, sardonyx, sardius, chrysolyte, beryl, topaz, chrysoprasus, jacinth and amethyst have an ancient symbolism, so that the numbers and colours meant something very real in St. John's day. We must beware of looking at apocalyptic writings as though they were the works of the deranged. It is ourselves who have lost the key to the language which would render them intelligible.

Jerusalem also appears as a celestial city in the *Epistle of Paul the Apostle to the Galatians*,[6] where he writes: 'Jerusalem which is above

---

[1] *The Ideal City* p. 18.
[2] *Ezekiel* Ch. 40.
[3] *Kings I* Ch. 6, 20.
[4] *The Revelation of St. John the Divine* Ch. 21, 16–22.
[5] *Ibid.* Ch. 21, 2.
[6] Chapter 4, 26.

us is free, which is the mother of us all.' Again the imagery of the city as a woman appears.

Jerusalem, holy city of the Jews, has now entered Christian writings as a symbol of the City of God, the bride, the mother. As Jerusalem grew in stature, so there was a reaction, in that images were found for the Citadel of Satan as a symbol of evil. Sodom and Gomorrah had for centuries been noted as cities of ill repute, and Babylon was added to the list of Infernal Cities.

From Judaeo-Christian traditions sprang the architectural image of a moral symbol. This development may have been aided by the fact that living things were not allowed to be represented pictorially.[1] In Christian churches and manuscripts Jerusalem, Rome and Bethlehem become symbolic of the City of God. The symbolic facets of the celestial city gave the Middle Ages a potent weapon which became a political force during the Crusades.

The Jews declined as a nation from the sixth century, and finally their land became a Roman province. The scattering of the Jews over the face of the earth after their defeat by Titus might have obliterated their culture, but their ancient customs, loyalty to the tribal group and traditions, and their belief in themselves as a superior race preserved their identity, so that they were always a highly significant people in all cultures and ages.

Christ was a crucial figure in Jewish history, for his message went beyond the Jews themselves to the world. His message was one of catholicity: it embraces all peoples and races. It is an extraordinary fact that the teachings of Jesus Christ and the myths and stories that were developed about Him dominated Europe for a millennium and a half. The domination of western life by the last of the great Jewish prophets can be seen today in the architectural dominants of towns and cities, and in the development of our whole culture.

[1] *The Ideal City* p. 20.

IV

The Empire of Rome

THE RISE AND FALL OF THE WESTERN EMPIRE

Rome was founded in the eighth century B.C. by the organization of tribal settlements on neighbouring hills into a political unit under an elected leader who acted as military commander, priest and judge. In the beginning, Roman farms were run by families, and were self-sufficient, but with the rise of a patrician class, their wealth gained in war and by reward, the plebeian or small family farmers became gradually less well-off, especially when the rising ruling class seized the common lands for their own needs.[1] This pauperization of the smallholders recalls the enclosure of lands in eighteenth century Britain.

At the beginning of the fifth century the plebeians became restive, and the revolutionary mood was such that the monarchy was replaced by a republic with two consuls as its leaders. The plebeians were granted political expression and the common lands were returned to the people. The republic developed an expansionist policy which created an insatiable demand for troops and fodder, as well as creating a national incentive to serve the army and work harder, since the political and economic rewards were so great. In the third century B.C. Rome extended her rule over the whole of Italy, incorporating the Hellenic city-states, and the various tribes and cultures fused together to form a new national consciousness.

A new upper class developed, namely the rich and successful patricians and plebeians, and with the rise to prominence of this class came capitalism on a huge scale. The ambitions and achievements of Roman power may be traced to the origins of the nation. The founders of a united Italy under Rome had solid earthy roots. They had drained and irrigated the land, built great aqueducts and buildings, and created a highly organized and peaceable society. Their fighting men were farmers who wielded their swords as deftly as their agricultural implements. The industry, sobriety and

[1] *History Builds the Town* p. 30.

strength of purpose of the Roman farming stock contrasted strongly with the decaying civilizations of the known world.

Hellenistic culture, overstretched and thinly spread, was in a state of dissolution; Egypt under the Ptolemies was a strange amalgam of watered-down civilizations; Persia and the Jews were no match for a self-confident and prospering military people. The only obstacle in the west to imperial ambition was Carthage, and it was conquered in 146 B.C. Rome became master of the Mediterranean, including the North African coast, Sardinia, Sicily, Greece, Asia Minor and Spain, and by A.D. 100 Rome was the centre of the known world.

Rome had neither a religion which was truly part of its culture, nor a philosophical tradition capable of dealing with the problems created by the Empire and the new influences absorbed into the Roman way of life. The religions and ideas from many conquered peoples were embraced willy-nilly. Mithras, Serapis, Isis, Osiris, and many others joined the Graeco-Roman gods and goddesses in the pantheon of Roman religion. Greek sculpture and art were collected by the rich, military and commercial power that was Rome. The Romans became connoisseurs rather than creators.

Rome established what the individual city-states had not been able to do: she gave the world peace and political institutions on a supranational scale. Law, administration, engineering, civic and military works covered the world as it was known then, yet Rome's lack of cultural invention made her a sponge, absorbing all that other civilizations had to offer, including a multiplicity of religious cults. The enormous expansion by conquest gave the Empire a huge slave population, while the merchants, traders and financiers grew richer through the provision of armaments, ships and fodder.

Slavery attached a stigma to manual work, and as slavery developed, the pressure to invent new methods and improve the technology slackened. Given an unlimited and cheap labour force, it was quite unnecessary to rationalize production methods or modernize techniques, but it was possible, on the other hand, to sustain a huge bureaucracy and an enormous expenditure on armaments and the military, if society were carried on the backs of a slave population. The slaves could be encouraged to more effort by permitting them to purchase their freedom, so incentives were provided for the main labour force.

Rome adopted the ideas and cultures of other less spiritually bankrupt civilizations, as well as forcing tribute from subject peoples. Rome was 'not a productive society, but a military robber state'.[1] Lewis Mumford states[2] that 'Roman culture was choked by its material advantages'.

It must be emphasized that a Roman was first of all a Roman citizen, which meant that he was a member of an urban community modelled on Roman law, administration and practice. *Roman*, in this sense, no longer meant *a citizen of the city of Rome*. In A.D. 212 Caracalla granted citizenship to all free members of the Empire.

The Roman Empire had a network of roads which survives to this day. They were straight, constructed for military use and for the avoidance of ambush. The Empire was strongly urbanized, and we can establish something of the imageability and inscape of Roman towns by studying the considerable physical remains of their culture.

The Empire was a super-efficient state at its zenith, with the most powerful army in the world. Civil life had to comply with military needs, and for the exercise of imperial control, all communications and services had to allow for speedy movement from one part of the Empire to another. The rigid and standardized planning of the Roman *castrum*, and later the fortified town, meant that military control could easily be re-established in times of trouble. The pre-Hippodamian towns of Hellenic culture were not ideal for the regaining of control and the imposition of order in the event of revolt, but they were splendid for guerilla warfare.[3] The Roman *castrum* had a standard plan so designed that the troops of the *Imperium Romanum* would be equally familiar with their surroundings and layout no matter in which part of the vast Empire they were stationed. The main axis of the *castrum* was the *Cardo Maximus* running north–south, and off it the various barracks and quarters could be reached by roads at right angles to the main street. Four gates, a wall and fortified towers completed the design of the *castrum*.

The great military, commercial, legal and administrative organization of Rome made for the uniformity of architectural design and construction throughout the Empire, emphasizing symbolically the wholeness and catholicity of imperial power. The towns, like the *castra*, were similar, having a 'pattern of straight streets, crossing at

[1] *History Builds the Town* p. 31.
[2] In *The Condition of Man* p. 39.
[3] Aristotle mentions this point in *Politics* VII, 1330b, p. 206.

right angles and enclosing rectangular blocks or *insulae.*'[1] Cecil
Stewart draws our attention to the ease of policing such a town as
well as its obvious economic advantages as it was very straight-
forward to map out. Such plans provided the Roman tax man with
a clear picture of the areas of building and road, and therefore of
areas of control. Hughes and Lamborn[2] mention the advantage of
this type of plan for postal addresses.

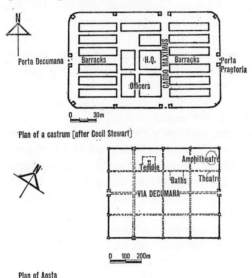

Plan of a castrum [after Cecil Stewart]

Plan of Aosta

Roman plans   Figure No. 14

It is interesting to note that when Roman towns were founded,
the extremities of it were marked with a plough pulled by a cow
and a bull.[3]

The use of rectangular plots, although attributed to Hippodamian technique, had earlier origins, for the augur, when seeking
guidance from the gods, marked off a square on the earth and
divided it into four, whereupon he studied the four quarters for
omens.[4] We have already mentioned the appearance and significance of squares in previous chapters.

[1] *A Prospect of Cities* p. 29.
[2] In *Towns and Town Planning* p. 9.
[3] *History Builds the Town* p. 32.
[4] *Towns and Town Planning* p. 6.

Towns usually had two main roads at right angles to each other: the *Decumanus* running east–west, and the *Via Principalis* or *Cardo* running north–south. These main streets were frequently colonnaded and enriched with arches and monuments, as at Timgad and Palmyra.

In all the Roman settlements, characteristic Roman remains are found. The process of assimilation which existed throughout the Empire gradually created unity out of diversity, politically and culturally. Although Latin was the official language, Greek remained the dominant tongue in the eastern part, while north African languages remained in use, even to the extent of appearing with Latin on inscriptions. Local languages remained in use throughout the life of the Empire.[1]

In architectural and civic design achievement, Hellenistic influences played a dominant rôle. The international reality of Hellenistic culture, and the cities, buildings and sculpture which existed had a tremendous influence on the Roman conquerors. Hellenistic culture, in terms of its artistic achievements, was such a force that even after the Empire in the west had dissolved, the qualities of the Eastern Empire were dominantly Greek in origin. The conquered lands of the west, however, did not exercise this influence, for the indigenous culture was in visual terms so underdeveloped that the essentially urban nature of the conquering system soon created aggressively Roman dominants unaffected by local qualities. The existing buildings in Nîmes and Arles bear this view out. Although the Celtic peoples fought ferociously, and did their best to stop the advancing imperial armies, they had not created the kind of architectural and urban forms which would impress a Roman. The dominantly Greek speaking population of the east, and the Hellenistic cities with their developed architecture and statuary managed to retain qualities of essentially Greek character even under the Roman Empire.

It is interesting to note that although Rome became a museum for antiquities, and informed connoisseurs prized much great classical sculpture, there seems to have been a lack of creative power in the Empire, which would account for the enormous numbers of copies of Greek originals. But although it is true that Rome never produced art to match that of the Greeks, except perhaps in the realm of portrait-sculpture, Hellenistic culture seems to have gone

[1] *Rome and her Empire* pp. 14 and 15.

through a non-inventive period as well. The last great Hellenistic sculptures, such as the Laocoön group, were apogees of creation – what might be described as Hellenistic baroque. The great altar at Pergamon is described by Kenneth Clark as 'an example of that inflated official art with which the nineteenth century made us familiar'.[1] The Laocoön group, however, he describes as 'the most influential of all embodiments of pathos'. The Laocoön group is a work of genius, rising above the pomposity of such a work as the Pergamon altar, and is an original work, unlike much contemporary art which consisted of copies of earlier works.[2] We see in the Laocoön[3] one of the most shattering expressions of pathos in all sculpture, and this is no accident, for it symbolizes the artistic consciousness which was protesting against the return to sterile copying of traditional form. Hellenistic culture generally, though, began the process of copying classical works which Rome was to adopt. Yet the originals had been created within the Zeitgeist of a particular epoch. They may have been religious in origin, and their existence symbolized the Zeitgeist of their own period. Copies of them, however, could not express the original spirit, but the very fact of their being copies symbolized the barrenness of the creative force.

The outward expansion, the Caesarism of the Romans, has been seen by many to be manifestations of their spiritual emptiness. It is not as easy as that. After the death of Alexander the Great and the subsequent vacuum in international power politics, it was natural that this vacuum had to be filled. It might have been Carthage, but it happened to be the new, virile and self-confident Rome that did so. The conquering power became the medium by which Greek art forms were distributed throughout the known world. Egyptian, Persian and eastern products were available too, but the connoisseurs of Rome seem to have prized the art of Greece above all. Roman temples were clothed in ornament derived from Greek examples, yet the structural techniques were entirely different. The Romans were superb engineers: they used the arch and they used concrete, yet they clothed their buildings in borrowed garments, transforming them in the process to something even more grandiose than Hellenistic developments of the orders of architecture. It is significant that the Romans preferred the Corinthian order to any other, and developed it themselves to a highly ornate Roman Corinthian order.

[1] *The Nude* p. 219.
[2] *Rome and her Empire* p. 18.   [3] *See Plate* 55.

The *pax Romana* was essentially a system of law and order backed up by a military machine, and the Zeitgeist was reflected in the design of the cities, with their triumphal ways, arches and victory columns. The size and uniformity of Roman power is physically expressed in the enormous network of roads and aqueducts; in the layout and details of the cities, which varied little throughout the Empire; and in the sculptured reliefs of triumphal arches and victory columns telling of military conquest in all corners of the known world. Yet as military and political triumphs were celebrated, so there were signs of a terrible disorder in the Roman soul.

From the rise of the Caesars, and their glorification in temples, mausolea and monuments, there is evidence of a growing malaise. The very nature of Roman rule seems to have become more vicious after the accession of Caligula in A.D. 37. The succeeding reigns of Claudius, Nero, the three emperors, followed by Vespasian and Titus, covering a time scale of only 44 years, were notable for the growth of public spectacle, inevitable wars, the conquest of central Britain, the great fire of Rome, the beginning of the persecution of the Christians, the destruction of Jerusalem and the Temple, the scattering of the Jews and the building of the Flavian amphitheatre which was to be the largest of its kind anywhere.

The growing tendency to keep the Roman proletariat amused by vast spectacles, usually of a bloody and degrading nature, dates from the rise of Caesarism, although the *Circus Maximus* had been in existence during the republican rule. The circuses and arenas were developed to offer release from the civic and military repression. In the amphitheatres and circuses, huge crowds could see death, revolting cruelty, danger, excitement, speed, warfare, combat and the destruction of human dignity, purely as spectators, without being further involved. The throwing of captives to the wild animals, gladiatorial combat and miniature wars possibly served as reminders to the people to behave, but soon developed into popular shows. The spectators were treated to organized brutality on an enormous scale, and, safe in their seats, protected by the high walls of the arena, were detached from it all: as detached as are the millions today who sit nightly in front of their television sets. They were, in a different sense, involved as well, for there was no end to the carnage; blood lust demanded more, and victims flocked to the execution in ever increasing numbers, as the emperor and his subjects insisted on more human sacrifices. Seneca saw the dangers of such shows, and indeed attacked slavery as well as brutality. It is not altogether surprising that Seneca held such opinions, for, in his day (he died in A.D. 65) not only was Christianity gaining ground, but there must have been many with roots in the old pagan traditions whose sensibilities were hanging in shreds in such a period.

The Baths, designed to cater for all tastes on as large and as magnificent a scale as possible, were monumental pleasure palaces for the people. The grossness and vulgarity of life under a succession of debauched emperors was distinctly mirrored in the coarse façadism of the public buildings of the time, glorying in richness, voluptuousness and enormity. The monuments, too, were unashamed and bombastic expressions of such events as the sacking and destruction of Jerusalem celebrated on the Arch of Titus. The proliferation of such buildings of pleasure, triumphal arches and monuments may be explained by the growth of the holiday as an institution. Since slavery was now universal, work for free citizens could practically stop altogether, until by the reign of Marcus Aurelius (A.D. 161–180) there were over 150 public holidays and spectacles per year. It was a form of bribery to keep the people drugged and sated. No free man went hungry either, for a 'public assistance board' organized the free issue of corn to the urban masses, so a kind of welfare state was set up to smooth over any rumblings of discontent.

Yet if the libraries, *thermae*, circuses, monuments and arenas were grandiose and magnificent, the housing for the proletariat was not, for they lived in jerry-built blocks of flats which had a high fire risk. In the reign of Augustus, legislation was introduced to check the dangers of fire and collapse by insisting that no new tenements should exceed 70 feet in height, and under Trajan this was reduced to 60 feet (A.D. 98–117).[1] The great fire of Rome in the reign of Nero (A.D. 64) is normally remembered for the imperial violin solo, but what is forgotten is that under Nero legislation was introduced to replace the bad layout and dangerous structures with soundly built dwellings fronted with stone and limited in height.

Under Nero many new schemes for the enrichment of the capital were started: broad streets with colonnades replaced many squalid alleys which were usually half blocked by beams shoring up the timber-framed tenements.

By the reign of Trajan, none but the richest could afford a house. The word *domus* came to mean nothing more than the best flat in

---

[1] *Towns and Town Planning* p. 20.

an apartment block. Villas were built in smaller towns and cities still, and, of course, in the country, but in the great metropolis tenements far outnumbered private houses.

Apart from the basic layout of Roman towns already mentioned, perhaps the most influential aspect of Roman civic design was the municipal dignity expressed in the fora of Roman towns. The most monumental of all fora was the *Forum Romanum* as it developed under the emperors Trajan, Hadrian, Antoninus Pius and Marcus Aurelius (A.D. 98–180). Principles of symmetry and axial planning providing great vistas; ostentatious and magnificent display; enrichment and glorification of each emperor produced the cluster of spaces, buildings and colonnades which comprised the greatly expanded *Forum Romanum*. Contrasted with the Hellenistic agora, the forum was completely symmetrical and axial in its later development. The sequences in Rome of the old *Forum Romanum*, fora of Vespasian, Nerva, Augustus, Julius Caesar and Trajan, culminating in the Ulpian Basilica and Temple of Trajan created a monumental civic centre which expressed on every hand the glory of the emperors. On axes in each forum were the Temples of Peace, Minerva, Mars Ultor, Venus Genetrix and Trajan. Columns, statuary, altars and inscriptions enriched the spaces, while the great temple of Venus and Rome stopped the vista at one end of the *Via Sacra*, which separated the old forum from the new developments, and the Arch of Septimius Severus closed the other. Rome herself was glorified in the forum, and the emperors symbolized Rome, for they had dictatorial powers, could order life or death, held by far the greatest part of the wealth of the Empire, and were elevated to the status of gods themselves. Jupiter may have had a temple on the Capitoline hill, but the real dominants were the victory columns, arches, and reminders on every side of the power and majesty of the rulers.

Roman attitudes to architectural and civic design may be studied in the work of Vitruvius. His *De Architectura*, written in the reign of Augustus Caesar, reflects the political climate of his day. Vitruvius devoted much attention to building for the politically dominant members of society, while social questions remained, for him, unimportant. Civic design, formality, structure and town planning were considered by Vitruvius. The markets of the town were to be situated centrally in inland towns, but near the harbour in the case of a port. In discussing town planning as a whole, however, he draws our attention to defence, the arrangement of streets, the positioning of dwellings according to social position and wealth, and to the requirements of merchants and commercial interests. The Vitruvian city was to be enclosed by an octagonal wall, and eight streets were to run to the centre between the directions of line of the eight prevailing winds. The predominance of eight in the Vitruvian scheme of things was based on ancient belief.[1] The Tower of the Winds in Athens (100–35 B.C.), also known as the Horologium of Andronikos Cyrrhestes, was an octagonal building on a stylobate of three steps, and the eight sides faced the most important points of the compass. It was dedicated to eight deities. In divination rites, sixteen or double eight was a significant number.[2] 'The meaning of these rites . . . emphasizes the relation between man and the universe,' states Dr. Rosenau, in *The Ideal City*, and she mentions the sub-division of the Vitruvian plan into segments of eight and sixteen as being significant. It would appear to the present writer that the Vitruvian ideal plan is, in fact, based on a mandala form, and on ideas of perfection, harmony and order. The sub-division of the city plan with eight or sixteen segments differs from Platonic conceptions of magic numbers which we have already mentioned in Chapter III.

If there had been signs of spiritual exhaustion in the Empire, physical signs of danger threatening appeared in the reign of Aurelianus (A.D. 270–276) when the great defensive walls were erected round Rome. For half a millennium, Rome was defended at the frontiers of her Empire, now suddenly the Empire was under serious attack. Athens was sacked by invaders in A.D. 292, and in A.D. 293 the Empire was divided into four parts, each ruled separately. The four courts placed a great financial burden on the state.

The power of Rome rested on her army, and yet, as the centuries passed, the army became less Roman and therefore less loyal to Rome. Money talks, and the man who paid the army had the loyalty of the soldiers. In the third century, anarchy developed, accentuated by wars, plagues, the claims of rival factions to the throne, and by the army getting further involved in a power struggle between various pretenders. Scapegoats had to be found, and the Christians were hunted out with increased savagery from the reign of Decius (A.D. 249–251).

The establishment of the Tetrarchy, when Diocletian reigned with three others, also saw the reorganization of the army so that

[1] *The Ideal City* p. 15.
[2] *Ibid.* p. 15.

allied forces were stiffened with 'reliable' troops and a secret police force was introduced, that inevitable instrument of totalitarianism. Since the Goths, Saxons, Alamans, Franks and Vandals were now forming highly organized military forces, it was essential to stop their incursions. These peoples wanted a place in the sun, and a share in the wealth of the Empire. They were also being pushed west and south by other eastern peoples such as the Huns. After the sacking of Ephesus and Athens by the Goths, the new political climate was one of uncertainty and fear. The emperor Valerianus had died as a slave in Persia, and another emperor, Valens, was to die in battle in A.D. 378. This climate determined that since Rome was no longer safe, its function as a capital would cease to be important, especially since Diocletian left it to rule from his fortress-palace at Split.[1] After the abdication of Diocletian and Maximian as Augusti, the two Caesars, Constantius and Galerius became Augusti, and Severus and Daia became Caesars.[2] Various factions put up other candidates, and for nineteen years armies fought and politicians intrigued, until Constantine emerged as sole emperor in A.D. 324, although he had been proclaimed Augustus in A.D. 306, and Rome ceased to be the capital of the Empire.

Rome had, under successive emperors, gradually declined in importance. Political transformation was succeeded by changes in religion. Old gods were giving ground to new ones, such as Mithras, and Christianity was everywhere gaining converts. With the centralization of power in the person of the emperor, the centre of the *Imperium Romanum* was where the emperor chose to be. During the Tetrarchy this is borne out by the sudden importance and subsequent enrichment of such towns as Trier, Salonika and Split, all imperial capitals at that time. As the political and cultural heart of the Empire shifted, Rome became less important, since its traditions, based on republicanism and the rise of the Roman state became less and less relevant to the political climate at the end of the third century. Rome became a constant source of expense and trouble, being too close to the collapsing frontiers. Christianity was going from strength to strength, and, since the partial recognition by Constantine at the beginning of the fourth century, had become a major force.

Christianity was, in a sense, a mystery religion, as entry was by

[1]   *The End of the Roman World* p. 52.
[2]   *Augustus* was the title of the emperor, while *Caesar* came to signify the vice-emperor.

baptism. It also, in the course of its first three hundred years, absorbed much pagan custom and belief into its fabric, as well as identifying with the infinitely older beliefs of Judaism. Jewish morality and history remained an essential part of the structure of Christian belief. The Church survived persecution because in its early days it was decentralized and existed in tiny pockets throughout the Empire and beyond it. Greek philosophers used their own traditions of logic and reason to promulgate Christian belief, and logic and magic were reconciled in an entity which became the dogma of the Church. 'Theology,' states Mumford, 'was as much a Greek invention as philosophy.'[1]

Just as Rome had absorbed many cults, gods and goddesses, and established them in its pantheon, so Christianity adapted and incorporated much pagan belief, so that a wholesale Christianizing of Roman civilization was not as unlikely as would at first appear. There had been traditions going back to Stoicism and to Jewish apocalyptic visions which would have paved the way to some extent. The emperor Marcus Aurelius had been a Stoic, and his fatalism was echoed in the attitudes of Christian anchorites in the deserts of Nubia. The negation of worldly life and the pessimism of the Zeitgeist were accentuated by the predatory incursions by the barbarian invaders.

The autocrats of the Empire realized that if a means could be found of uniting State and Church, Christians might be as ready to die for the emperor as they had hitherto died for Christ. After the emergence of Flavius Valerius Constantinus, known as Constantine the Great, as emperor, a huge statue of him was erected in Rome. On his head was a helmet with the *chi-rho* (XP)[2] monogram inscribed on it, and thus Christ officially took the place of the old gods. This was because Constantine had won a battle in which his troops carried the monogram on their shields. Since Christ had now taken a direct hand in the fortunes of the emperor, and therefore of the Empire, the new religion was recognized and incorporated into the state. The colossal statue shows for the last time the exaltation of the emperor into an equal of the gods.[3] The fragments of this statue existing today show us that the powers of creation were not dead: the hand alone is a noble piece of carving, and the fragment of an arm suggests Michelangelo.

[1] *The Condition of Man* p. 66.
[2] *chi-rho*. The first two letters of the Greek *Christos*.
[3] *Rome and her Empire* pp. 208–211.

After Constantine moved his capital to Byzantium, Rome declined rapidly in importance, yet show and pomp remained a part of daily life there well into the fourth century.[1] The great engineering works such as the aqueducts, bridges and roads were so strongly built that little repair was needed, but the spirit of a capital city was departing.

Wars, invasions and political strife heralded the new century where, throughout the Empire, Christianity, 'that quaint Alexandrian *tutti-frutti*,' as Norman Douglas somewhat scathingly referred to it,[2] was triumphant. The Council of Nicaea (A.D. 325) had decided what was heresy and what was not, and laid down a party line for religion which, by the dawn of the fourth century, was a dominant force in life. The Flavian amphitheatre ceased having gladiatorial shows in A.D. 404 and the city of Rome by this date must have only been a shadow of its former self, since Constantine had ransacked it for ornaments to dignify his jerry-built capital at Byzantium. It was not only the ornaments, however, that had been taken, but the craftsmen, statesmen, scholars and artists too.

When Alaric and his armies finally took Rome in 410, the city cannot have lived up to his expectations. Gibbon leads us to look upon the event as a singular disaster, but Alaric was a Christian, in search of a home and food for his people, and the damage he did must have been little compared with the ravages of Constantine and his successors.

The real damage to the Empire caused by the capture of Rome was not material, but spiritual: it was a traumatic experience from which the Empire never recovered. Alaric, in fact, only spent a few days in Rome before going on in desperation to seek corn for his people. A tribe in search of food and a place to settle does not carry enormous quantities of loot about with it. Orosius tells us of the piety of Alaric and the respect in which he held the shrines. He died before 410 was out, a disappointed man, but certainly not the monster he has been thought of by so many for so long.

After Constantine there were two emperors and occasionally one. Rome became an occasional capital of the Western Empire. Ravenna had for a time been the seat of power, but the Western Empire from the reign of Honorius (A.D. 395–423) to Romulus Augustulus (A.D. 475–476) was in a more or less permanent state of political

[1]   *The Condition of Man* p. 81.
[2]   In *Old Calabria* p. 323.

collapse. The western Roman Empire ended when the German king Odovacer captured the last emperor, Romulus Augustulus, son of Orestes, who was adviser to Attila the Hun.

THE EASTERN EMPIRE

Byzas had founded Byzantium in the seventh century B.C. after consulting the Delphic Oracle about the site. The city grew as a trading centre, and possessed strategic importance, a natural harbour and a geographically significant position in the Greek world. It was fortified with a wall and a citadel on the acropolis. Alexander the Great captured the city and used it as a base for his imperialist adventures. Septimius Severus laid siege to and took Byzantium in A.D. 194, and transformed it into a Roman provincial city with hippodrome, baths and palaces.

In A.D. 324 Constantine became sole emperor and, in the following year Christianity became the state religion. Byzantium became Constantinople and the capital of the first Christian Empire. New fortifications were erected, and the area of the city was trebled. A magnificent forum was built, with colonnades around it, archways at each end, and a huge column in the centre. From the top of this column, as a gigantic statue, Constantine watched over his city. Now this statue was by Phidias and had originally been of Apollo to whom Byzantium had once been dedicated.[1] Constantine had the statue transformed, so Apollo and Constantine, tradition and modernity, past and present, emerged in the one symbol.

Five fora along the length of the Mesé from the Hippodrome to an arch in the wall of Constantine near the Sea of Marmora comprised the foci for social and commercial life. Churches were built in numbers after A.D. 325. The Hippodrome was enlarged, and 2 theatres, 8 public and 153 private baths, 52 porticos, 5 granaries, 8 aqueducts or cisterns, 14 churches, 14 palaces, 4388 houses, and 4 basilicas were built in the six years after Constantine decreed the city should be his capital.[2]

Yet certain aspects of the selection of Byzantium as a capital are puzzling. Although Diocletian had founded a palace at Split, and another at Nicomedia opposite Byzantium, and although the heart of the Empire had moved eastwards, Constantine's long-term political aims are hard to assess. He had fought ferocious wars to re-unify

[1] *City of Constantine* pp. 4 and 5.
[2] *Ibid.* p. 11.

the Empire, yet he himself divided it again. Apart from geographical location, there was another powerful motive for siting the capital at Byzantium, and that was the honouring of the lands of Illyricum after its soldiers and people had saved the Empire. Constantine had originally thought of Sofia, in modern Bulgaria, as his capital[1] which in any case was to express and symbolize the new conditions in state, religion and life. Thus a site had to be selected which was free of tradition, and so with a new Zeitgeist and a new site as well as a new city, a new civilization emerged which some have called Byzantinism.

The ruling classes of the Byzantine Empire were all subservient to one despot – the emperor. This despotism was enhanced by the union of Church and State; orthodoxy replaced morality, and in art and architecture a Byzantine style developed which remained relatively unchanged throughout the following centuries.

The desire to build is strong in despots, for there is nothing more symbolic of tremendous political power than monumental building on as large a scale as possible carried out in the minimum of time.

It was God who told Constantine to select a site other than Ilium which he had decided upon previously.[2] This would seem to be a Christian version of Apollonian tales and the utterances of the Delphic Oracle. According to Burckhardt, Constantine traced the outlines of the walls of the city with his spear, and on being asked if the journey would be much farther replied that he would proceed until 'he who walks before me stops'. The foundation of the west wall was ceremonially celebrated in A.D. 326, shortly after Crispus Caesar, Constantine's son and heir, was executed on the orders of his father.

The city was named in A.D. 330, and the event was celebrated with pageants and games. Thereafter, on the anniversary of the date of dedication, an image of Constantine was carried through the Circus together with the traditional figure of Tyche. Constantine covered the city with monuments to himself, and it is not surprising that he himself became a cult.[3]

Constantinople obtained an immigrant population by command of the emperor, and artists, builders and craftsmen were ordered to proceed at once to the new capital. Roman senators were brought from the old capital, and a senate house was built, but it remained

---

[1]   *The Age of Constantine the Great* p. 344.
[2]   *Ibid.* pp. 346–347.
[3]   *The Age of Constantine the Great* p. 349.

a mere charade, with little or no power. Other cities gave their citizens up to Constantinople by coercion, and Jerome remarked that Constantinople was clothed in the nudity of other cities. While he was principally referring to population, he must also have had taxation and physical looting in mind. Many cities of the Empire were stripped of their treasures to glorify the new capital, and Constantine and his minions offended both pagans and Christians by plundering temples and churches to enrich Constantinople in his own name. Greek statues in their hundreds were brought to decorate the baths, fora and squares; portrait-statuary was carried from Rome and altered crudely in many cases to the likeness of the emperor. Burckhardt informs us that even a Tyche had been plundered from Rome, symbolizing the transfer of power and fortune to Constantinople, but a cross had been placed on her pagan brow. At a festival in A.D. 330, prayers to Tyche were intermingled with shouts of 'Kyrie eleison.'[1]

From Delphi came the serpentine column; from Rome came the bronze Greek horses from Nero's arch which now dignify St. Mark's in Venice; from all over the Empire came bits of temples, altars, statuary and paintings which were hurriedly erected as a stage-set for the Constantinian pomp and ceremonial.

Yet if the world power of Rome had shifted to Constantinople, the old capital still retained a potent advantage: it was the see of a bishop who held precedence over all others, and it possessed some of the greatest monuments of Imperial Rome. Throughout the third century, paganism produced the architectural dominants: the Baths of Caracalla, Diocletian and Constantine, and the monumental embellishments of the forum symbolize the Zeitgeist of the epoch. Libraries, fora, baths, amphitheatres, circuses, over thirty triumphal arches, hundreds of statues and victory columns dominated the city of Rome.

The luxurious life of the Romans helped to turn the Christians to asceticism, and a number of monasteries began to appear throughout the Empire at this time, encouraged, no doubt, by Jerome, who regarded celibacy as a requisite for spiritual life. The shores of the Mediterranean and the deserts became populated with anchorites.

As Christianity became more of a dominant force in the lives of

[1] A form of prayer in all the ancient Greek liturgies, absorbed into the Roman Catholic *Latin* mass, so that *Kyrie eleison* and *Christe eleison* are the only *Greek* words in the mass.

the people, so Jerusalem, Bethlehem and Nazareth became celestial cities: earthly-heavenly places of pilgrimage. They began to be adorned and enriched in the reign of Constantine, and the holy places became desirable areas for the retirement of the wealthy Christian upper classes. As Rome had been the scene of so many martyrdoms, so it gradually became a holy city for the Christians, and joined the cities of the Holy Land in the catalogue of heavenly cities.

A great shortage of architects in Constantinople in A.D. 334 made it necessary for a new law to be promulgated instituting schools for the instruction of students in the art of architecture,[1] but unfortunately this seems to have had little immediate effect, for of Constantine's city only fragments remain: it was so jerry-built anyway

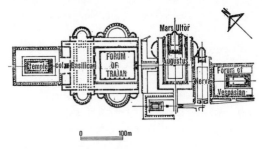

Roman Fora [after various sources]:

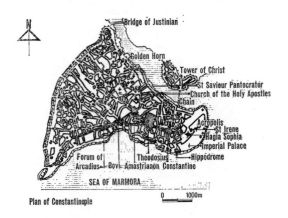

Plan of Constantinople

Roman plans   Figure No. 15

[1] *A Prospect of Cities* p. 41.

that it had to be almost entirely reconstructed in the first century of its life. However, the basic town plan had been laid out, and the sites for the major buildings had been established, including an arsenal on the site of the old acropolis. To the south of the acropolis was the Church of Hagia Sophia,[1] and then the imperial palace. Near the western gate was the Church of the Holy Apostles which was to be the mausoleum of the emperors.

Constantine had saved the Empire and adopted a religion which was to dominate European minds for over 1200 years. He established a despotism and a new aristocracy which replaced the Roman senatorial system of political delegation of power. After Rome had fallen to the Visigoths, then Vandals and Ostrogoths, Constantinople became infinitely more significant as the capital: Augustine even suggests that it, as capital of the Roman Empire, was singled out as the citadel for the protection of the Empire of Christ. As State and Church became one, so holidays were based on the religious calendar; contracts were solemnly sealed with the Cross; a misdemeanour in civil law became synonymous with heresy, and wars became exercises in religious zeal. The emperor was crowned by the patriarch, yet he appointed the patriarch who, curiously, represented a force which the emperor could not oppose without criticism.

Constantinople developed under Constantius and Theodosius the Great, the latter being responsible for the erection of the great fortifications. The city walls were maintained compulsorily by all the citizens, and were magnificent examples of military engineering.[2]

The focus of the Empire was at that point where Hagia Sophia, the Palace and the Hippodrome stood, representing symbolically the Deity, the emperor and the people. The Hippodrome was, in a sense, the true political centre of Constantinople, for it was here that the people met to air their opinions. In the reign of Anastasius (A.D. 491–518), feelings grew so strong that riots broke out, and a fire raged in the city which did much damage. Theoretically the Hippodrome had no practical significance in terms of day-to-day passing

---

[1] In many books this is referred to as *Santa Sophia*, which is incorrect. The church was *not* dedicated to *Saint Sophia*, but to *Hagia Sophia*, or *Holy Wisdom*. It may also be referred to, correctly, as *Sancta Sophia*. The church built in Constantine's reign was, of course, not the present structure, which is much later.

[2] *A Prospect of Cities* p. 45.

of laws, but it acted as a brake, for public opinion could be voiced there, and, in the case of an emperor leaving no heir, it gave supreme power, for the emperor was elected in the Hippodrome. A policy statement by the ruler was read to the people assembled there, where normally there would be spectacular shows, theatricals or races, and it would be booed or cheered accordingly. In a state which was almost completely totalitarian, free speech nevertheless existed, perhaps as a relic of Greek democracy.

The Hippodrome extensions were among the very first buildings to be completed in Constantinople. Afterwards the palace was sited to the south and east of it, and thus when Justinian came to build the new Hagia Sophia in 532–537, it was not orientated as it should have been, but had an inclination to the south-east. The Hippodrome thus influenced the design of the focal point of Constantinople and of the Empire in that because of its enormous size, it forced the Palace to follow a certain form, as well as influencing the orientation of the church and the layout of the immediate environs of the city. The axis of the Hippodrome ran through Hagia Sophia and stopped on the acropolis. Walls separated the Palace from the Hippodrome, partly, no doubt, to give the emperor a modicum of privacy, but mostly, one suspects, to protect the imperial person and belongings from a hostile people whipped into anger by orators in the Hippodrome.

Hagia Sophia was the architectural dominant after Justinian's reign (527–565). It was a monument as much to the Church as to the person of the emperor who was God's second-in-command on earth. When Justinian said he had surpassed Solomon, he made an understatement, for the mighty dome covered a church that was the finest and largest in Christendom. It too, however, was largely composed of plundered parts, for Justinian rifled the temples of the classic world to further his glory. The temple of Artemis at Ephesus gave up its columns, as did the temple of Jupiter at Baalbek; shrines at Delos, Cyzacus and even the Parthenon itself were looted to provide ready made parts for Justinian's new church.[1] Yet as a zenith in Byzantine art, Hagia Sophia is uncontested, for it was a fusing of Roman structural technique and pomp, Greek craftsmanship and sensibility, eastern mysticism and Christian symbolism. Hagia Sophia symbolized the City of God of which Augustine had written in the fourth century. The City of God was no Utopia, but

---

[1] *City of Constantine* p. 70.

Plate 21: Arch of Titus, Rome. (Mansell Collection.)

Plate 22: Parthenon, Athens. (Mansell Collection.)

Plate 23: Roman Walls at Venta Silurum (Caerwent).

Plate 24: In the shadow of the town, or market church, at Landsberg-am-Lech.

Plate 25: Landsberg-am-Lech. The town church.

Plate 26: Salzburg. The fortress of the Prince-Bishop from the forecourt of the Cathedral.

Plate 27: Salzburg. The palace of the Prince-Bishop dominates the town.

Plate 28: Norwich. The Cloisters.

Plate 29: Street sequence at Solbad Hall. The narrow medieval street is dominated by the tower of the church.

Plate 30: Street sequence at Solbad Hall. The town church dominates the town centre.

Plate 31: Street sequence at Solbad Hall. Even at normal eye level a chapel in the shadow of the church dominates. These three pictures demonstrate the subtle changes of scale which ensured that the church was the dominant both from a distance and at close quarters.

Plate 32: Lichfield, Staffordshire. The Cathedral.

Plate 33: Haarlem. The town centre.

Plate 34: Oxford. St. Mary's tower and spire.

Plate 35: *Magdalen College tower, Oxford.*

Plate 36: *Merton Street, Oxford.*

Plate 37: Town Hall (1484) and tower of the Church at Michelstadt, Odenwald.

Plate 38: Aachen. The Cathedral.

Plate 39: Aachen. The choir (1353–1413).

Plate 40: Lübeck. Holstentor in the foreground and Marienkirche on the left.

Plate 41: Rothenburg-ob-der-Tauber. Town gate and watchtower.

Plate 42: Rothenburg-ob-der-Tauber. Town gate and watchtower.

Plate 43: Rothenburg-ob-der-Tauber. Markusturm and Roderbrunnen.

Plate 44: Delft. The Nieuwe Kerk (1381) which faces the Landshuis across the square.

*Plate 45: Delft. Facing the Nieuwe Kerk is the Landshuis
of 1520.*

*Plate 46: Delft. The civic building and the Nieuwe Kerk
balance in importance.*

Plate 47: The canal at Delft looking towards the Oudekerk.

Plate 48: Solbad. Medieval Street.

Plate 49: Amsterdam – houses on the canal.

Plate 50: Carpaccio. Life of St. George. (*Mansell Collection.*)

Plate 51 : Pope Alexander VI (Mansell Collection.)

Plate 52 : Savonarola. (Mansell Collection.)

in fact was the Christian Church symbolized as a city for which men were to prepare for citizenship.

Constantinople was a city of stark contrasts, for there were great churches, magnificent palaces and public buildings, chariot ways, monumental squares and thriving commercial quarters, yet the squalor was sickening.[1] Contrasted with the houses of the aristocrats and favourites of the court, which faced the Sea of Marmora, were the miserable back streets of the poorer areas near the Golden Horn. In Constantinople the façades came first; the dwellings were filled in later.

Laws were made to try to improve the streets in the fifth century, but the wooden shacks of the poor were difficult to control. Shantytowns always defy regulation, and minimum by-laws did little to alleviate the squalor behind the magnificence.

Constantinople possessed huge reservoirs, many of them underground. The fact that the city was short of natural water supplies anyway made these necessary, but they were doubly needed since the capital was prone to attack.

Churches and monasteries abounded, for religion had become a part of everyday life. Constantinople was the capital of a Christian Empire which saw itself as the champion of the Christian faith. The visible signs of religion were everywhere, from shrines at street corners to the great church of Hagia Sophia.[2] The monks were held in deep respect, and they exercised a profound influence over the daily life of the people. The significance of Constantinople as a City of God was enhanced by the extraordinary number of sacred relics enshrined there.

Under Justinian, the feverish building activity expressed the power of the autocrat in a renewed way. Justinian attempted to outshine Imperial Rome by enriching his own capital. He defeated the Vandals in Africa, the Ostrogoths in Italy, and re-imposed the rule of the Empire in Spain. To celebrate his conquests and symbolize the reborn greatness of the New Rome, he erected churches all over the Empire as well as forts, walls and monasteries. It must not be forgotten that he was credited as the source and master-mind behind all the buildings in his dominions.

It is interesting to see the subtle change as time progressed in the relationship of the emperor to the state. After Justinian, the Church

---

[1] *Cities of Destiny* p. 162.
[2] *Byzantine Architecture and Decoration* pp. 22–23.

became the analogue of the Empire and its unity, and the Church even rose above the State as a power. In the process, however, it became in its turn totalitarian, falling victim to dogmatism and hair splitting metaphysical argument. Dissenters were exterminated, a retrograde step compared with the traditions of classical Greece. The wholesale adoption of Christianity by the people contaminated the meaning of the Christian religion,[1] for the cults of relics tended to satisfy the still pagan souls of the populace as well as the rapacity of the relic-suppliers.

Byzantine Christianity appears to have been an oppressive force, imposing its dogma and orthodoxy in place of influencing morality. From the ninth century empire, state and orthodoxy were one and the same, since orthodoxy was now the chief supporter of the Empire, serving it as a channel of opposition to the Frankish and Latin influences of the western church and peoples.

In the seventh century the Persians once again menaced the Empire, but after they had been defeated, Arabic peoples overran much of the imperial lands. Under Leo III and Constantine V, however, the Arabs were defeated and driven out of Anatolia, while the Bulgars were similarly held at bay. During this period, the character of the Empire changed, as Greek replaced Latin as the official language, and many succeeding emperors of Asiatic or Armenian descent occupied the imperial throne.

In the eighth century a crucial schism developed, as the Eastern Empire became more oriental and Rome, as capital of the ecclesiastical world in the west, tended to look more to the Franks for protection. The Papacy became a secular state in the mid-eighth century, and relations between west and east were further strained by the coronation of Charles the Great as emperor of the west in A.D. 800.

The hegemony of Constantinople over the Mediterranean was lost when the Normans conquered southern Italy and the Turks overran Asia Minor. The immense fortifications of the city preserved it until, ironically, this Christian capital fell to the Venetians and the Crusaders in 1204, the latter having been diverted from their fourth crusade by lures of loot. The destruction was monstrous and the pillage frightful: an act of such barbarity can scarcely be paralleled. The rule of the Crusaders and Venetians, known euphemistically as the Latin Empire, lasted 50 years, during which

---

[1] *Reflections on History* pp. 126–127.

the population of the city dropped by two-thirds and huge areas of it became desolate. Everything that could be taken was taken.[1]

The scholars and craftsmen had played their parts in preserving the legacies of Greece and Rome. The western adventurers destroyed Constantinople, leaving only the stripped churches, the walls, and a decimated and ruinous city. The palace became uninhabitable and the relics of the holy places were scattered all over Europe. Weakened by the horrors of the early thirteenth century and subsequent plagues, Constantinople was captured by the Turks on May 29th, 1453, when Constantine XI was cut down with the remains of his army. He had made a last appeal to rally Europe to his aid against the Turkish invasion, an appeal that was ignored practically, although prayers were offered instead. The long-term political effects were not considered at the time, and it was not until Prince Eugen and John Sobieski defeated the Turks at Vienna in the late seventeenth century that the Turkish incursions into Europe came to an end.

[1] *Cities of Destiny* p. 165.

V

The Middle Ages

INTRODUCTION

Between the collapse of the western Roman Empire and the eighth century lies a time known as the 'Dark Ages': a period of social, political and urban breakdown. The old Roman towns declined, fell into disrepair and any sense of political organization disappeared. The Saracens moved across from the east, the Northmen harassed the coasts, and tribes of Goths, Saxons, Angles, Jutes, Pomeranians, Vandals and Huns came in successive waves over various parts of Europe.

Italy became surrounded by barbarian kingdoms, and itself became part of the Ostrogoth kingdom of Theodoric. To the north were Burgundians and Alamans, and to the north again were the Franks, Frisians and Saxons. In Britain, the cities and towns which had been integral parts of the Roman system of government were abandoned or decayed as tribes of Angles, Saxons, Jutes and Frisians overran the remnants of Romano-British civilization. Christianity was replaced by Nordic gods, and the symbols of civilization, the towns, cities and villas, were destroyed by the invaders. Only gradually did the newcomers form settlements, for after the collapse of the Roman Empire in the west, society became dominantly rural, not least in Britain which had less urban culture than the rest of continental Europe even under Rome.

In Britain, the Anglo-Saxon invaders consisted initially of one-class tribes of farmer-warriors. Land was cultivated in plots, and two or three fields were given over to arable farming. Each year one of the fields would lie fallow, and so the pattern of English mediaeval farming was established. In addition, there was common land which was divided annually by lot.[1] Rough grazing was obtainable in the woods. Each village was open and not readily defended, and with the increase in population and the unsettled political climate, specialists in defence and warfare emerged who

---

[1] *A Prospect of Cities* p. 58.

protected the security of the settlements. This new class in Britain became the thanes who created defensive halls and stockades and possessed the heavy armour, with the result that they tended to dominate the rest of society. In Anglo-Saxon life, two classes developed: namely the thanes or war-lords who collected tributes from the rest of the tribes and so became even more powerful; and the *ceorls*, who farmed the land and took up arms under the leadership of the thanes in times of trouble. The domination of the tribes by a military caste, together with the agricultural pattern, were the beginnings of the feudal system. The warlike Saxons had no reason to form towns larger than small settlements of 100 families or so, and these were grouped round the hall of the chief thane. Initially, each member of the tribe had a right to farm, but with the concentration of power in the hands of a powerful minority, the rest of the community had to pay fixed dues and give military service in return for the privilege of using the land. Ultimately, the system became nation-wide, with a greater superstructure of nobles, aristocrats and finally a king, all carried on the backs of an increasingly less free peasantry.

In continental Europe, however, urban civilization was not dead, though it was decidedly sick. The Visigoths, Franks, Vandals and Ostrogoths who ruled Spain, France, North Africa, the Sicilies, and Italy were less anti-urban than the barbarian invaders of Britain. Many Roman towns became barbarian capitals, for the Gothic tribes at any rate had treated Roman cities with respect, and looked on the south as a Promised Land, just as the south has had a fascination for their descendants. The cold north and the cultured, sensual south have been dominant ideas in European minds for centuries:

> *Kennst du das Land, wo die Zitronen blühn,*
> *Im dunkeln Laub die Gold-Orangen glühn . . .?.*[1]

After the overthrow of the last emperor of the west, Romulus Augustulus, Odovacer became master of Italy. It is significant that Odovacer sought formal recognition from Constantinople, and he reigned as king of Italy from A.D. 476–489. He also showed his respect for the Papacy, and Pope Simplicius recognized the authority of this Ostrogothic king.

---

[1] 'Do you know that land where the lemon-trees bloom,
And golden oranges glow in the dark leaves . . .?'
(Johann Wolfgang von Goethe – *Mignon's Song*)

Odovacer was overthrown by Theodoric, and, curiously, it seems that Theodoric the Goth ruled his kingdom with justice and devotion. He was on the throne for 32 years, during which he revived games and races, repaired the aqueduct of Ravenna, built palaces and baths, walls and an amphitheatre. Under Theodoric, order and civilized rule were restored to Italy, and Goth and Roman seem to have lived at peace together under the monarchy. He was responsible for a programme of restoration and enrichment of Rome itself, although he had his capital at Ravenna which he dignified with many buildings. His tolerance was such that when an anti-Semitic purge took place in Ravenna in A.D. 523, he ordered the Roman Catholics to rebuild the synagogues and Jewish property at their own expense. Theodoric was an Arian, and therefore less anti-Semitic than the Roman Catholics, since the latter held the Jews guilty for Christ's crucifixion. The clash with the Roman Catholics, however, prompted the Emperor Justin to order the closure of all Arian churches in Constantinople, and an enraged Theodoric retaliated by imprisoning the Pope, who died in captivity. Chaos resulted, for Arian was ranged against Roman Catholic, Goth against Roman, and the Kingdom itself against the Empire. Lombardic allies of the emperor invaded Italy, and Rome was attacked. The weakened peninsula was subsequently overrun by Franks, Germans, Saracens, Normans and finally by Spaniards and Austrians.[1] Theodoric's great tomb at Ravenna, however, is an eloquent symbol of the power and dignity of the man who, for a while, united Roman and barbarian culture under his rule.

If the lemon trees of Mignon's song express the yearning for the South, it was Christianity which shed light and warmth on the northerners' beliefs. Wotan and the gods were to be destroyed and the world with them, not as in *Götterdämmerung* with the promise of redemption through love, but utterly and finally. The adoption of Christianity by the northern tribes was therefore understandable because the southern religion was one of belief in an eternal God and eternal life, a stark contrast to the pessimistic beliefs of the north.[2]

The primacy of the Bishop of Rome ensured a dominant role for Italy and its culture in the history of the Roman Catholic west. The

---

[1] *The End of the Roman World* pp. 106–107.
[2] It is fascinating to study the elements of Christian thought in Wagner's *Ring*, and how ideas of Redemption and Love temper the Nordic myth.

Christian ethic as expressed by Augustine gave a new significance to the family, to human life and to the dignity of women. This ethic pervaded life, and circuses and spectacles were gradually replaced in the west by the pomp and ceremonial of the Church, while the law itself changed so that mercy tempered justice. Under Pope Gregory the Great, the Papacy grew to a hierarchy of centralized ecclesiastical power, including financial, material and therefore political influence. The Church took over the functions of social welfare and education as the secular states declined, until it became a highly political force with a bureaucracy and taxation system of its own.

In the far northern lands, in Iona, Lindisfarne and Jarrow, Celtic monks fled from the barbarians and formed isolated seats of learning, while in Ireland, scholarly settlements developed in Bangor, Glendalough and Lough Erne, which kept the lamp of intellectual endeavour lit during a dark and troubled period. Missionaries went forth from these centres to spread the Gospel throughout the world, but it was not until the end of the sixth century that the Roman Church was re-established in Southern England with the founding of the Episcopate of Canterbury under Augustine.[1] This changed Saxon society, for Roman law was re-introduced, and the Church founded central control, written charters and legacies. Stone building techniques were revived, and in time the Church extended its influence over the whole country, dividing it into sees which were sub-divided into parishes normally coinciding with the Anglo-Saxon settlements.[2]

After the Danish incursions a new type of settlement was introduced with stockades and earthworks, and many old Roman fortifications were repaired. The Vikings introduced new forms of warfare so that the building of castles became essential and the rural communities became more and more subservient to the local lord.

The Frankish tribes in Europe had settled originally in isolated homesteads. Like the Saxons, however, and for similar reasons, a ruling class emerged of warriors, while the majority became serfs. The symbolic expressions of the power of these dominant classes were the buildings associated with them, and these later became potential nuclei of towns.

With the baptism of Clovis, King of the Franks, the influence of the Church grew in France and the Rhineland from the end of the

[1] *Augustine of Canterbury,* not *Augustine of Hippo.*
[2] *History Builds the Town* p. 38.

fifth century, until it reached the position of true catholicity of power as symbolized in the great stone churches of the Carolingian period.

Roman settlements revived gradually, and with the centralization of organization into bishoprics many towns grew in importance politically and commercially. The conversion of much of Central Europe by Anglo-Saxon and Irish monks such as Boniface and Colman encouraged the growth of settlements such as St. Gallen, Augsburg and many others as seats of monastic learning and commerce. The Church became the owner of huge areas of land, and by far the greatest political organization.

Charles the Great had ambitions to revive the Empire in the west, and when the Frankish lands had grown to a powerful state, Charles was crowned *Imperator Augustus* in A.D. 800 and his empire later became the Holy Roman Empire, a title which was not to become extinct until the nineteenth century. The extension of the Frankish kingdom and the elevation of its king to an imperial throne was possible through the rise of a warrior class of professionals, who had to be paid. Consequently, Church lands were confiscated to meet the demands of the military, and the newly constituted Empire came into conflict with the Church, a pattern which was to recur throughout the centuries.

In many cases, as we have seen, cities grew again in Europe because of the siting of a bishopric within an earlier settlement, such as a *castrum* or old Roman *civitas*. Centralization of power and external threat coagulated settlements into larger units, and older foundations were re-inhabited. Roman walls were restored, and walls were erected round monastic buildings. Holy places, such as the burial places of martyrs, became places of pilgrimage. Churches were first erected over or near the tombs of martyrs, so that the next step was the reverse process of burying the dead where convenience and growing prosperity caused the erection of churches. Eminent princes and churchmen were buried in the church as a privilege and the custom grew so that the practices of the few became extended to the burials of the many. 'The emanations from the bodies of Saints exercised a peculiar virtue upon all those who lay near them.'[1]

Mediaeval society was centred on the church. The original church of a town often became the 'town church', and in Germany

---

[1] *London* Vol. IV, pp. 161–176.

became the market church, since the markets were held under its walls as at Augsburg, where commerce was carried on in the shadow of St. Ulrich's Church. The churches and monasteries were the great landowners of the Middle Ages, and ministered to the poor, built houses for them and, especially in Flanders, played an important part in furthering the growth of the town by encouraging commercial enterprise, building and the arts. The terms 'town church' and 'market church' are significant, for the church was the focus for worship, pageantry, education and art.[1]

Thus we see that the religious buildings were of enormous importance, for round them the urban centre developed. Ecclesiastical buildings formed the nuclei of many towns, and the establishment of bishoprics gave rise to the development of cities. The cathedral at the heart of the *civitas* became the chief centre for human activity

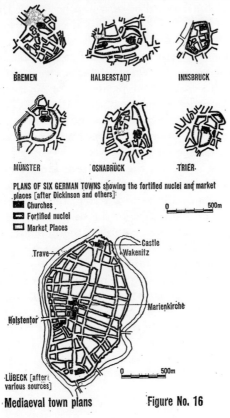

BREMEN   HALBERSTADT   INNSBRUCK

MÜNSTER   OSNABRÜCK   TRIER.

PLANS OF SIX GERMAN TOWNS showing the fortified nuclei and market places [after Dickinson and others]:
■ Churches
■ Fortified nuclei
□ Market Places

0   500m

Trave — Castle / Wakenitz

Marienkirche

Holstentor

LÜBECK [after various sources]

0   500m

Mediaeval town plans   Figure No. 16

[1] *The West European City* p. 255.

in artistic and commercial endeavour in much of Europe. In Germany, cathedrals were built on dominant walled sites, so that the city with its wall grew in turn round the central ecclesiastical stronghold. The church became associated with a citadel, and *Kloster* and *Burg* had double meanings, both literal and symbolic. It is no accident that the imagery of the church as a fortress pervades German mediaeval thought, as expressed in the chorale *Ein' feste Burg ist unser Gott*.[1] In England, the cathedral usually had a monastic origin, and so had cloisters, but it was always near a main secular settlement and fortification although it formed a separate precinct.

We have already mentioned the rise of a ruling secular class in the early Middle Ages, and the forming of camps or burghs as defensive forts against invaders. These burghs became the nuclei of secular administration and control of surrounding lands. In the Frankish kingdom and in Western Germany, hundreds of burghs were formed which developed into castles, and these became the houses of a powerful aristocracy. The settlements huddled round the castle for protection, and often the town fortifications were within the control of the castle. This ensured the protection of the town, but also enhanced the political dominance of the authorities in the castle.

The kings, dukes, prince-bishops and nobles held court in the urban settlements and many thus became capitals of independent states within a loose federal framework.

If originally it had been the bishops or kings who had directed that walls should be erected or older Roman walls should be rebuilt, it later became the prerogative of the townspeople to build and repair the city wall. Within the walls of the mediaeval town the structure of society was complex, the officials of both secular and ecclesiastical power exercising great authority, while the town councillors and members of the guilds came next in the hierarchy, followed by journeymen and apprentices. Under this superstructure were the peasants, who were little more than slaves. All, however, paid due respect to the Church, which was immensely rich and powerful, and it was the church which was the dominant building in the town.

If a wall could protect the town from invasions it could also protect the community from the 'protectors'. With the revival of

---

[1] Ascribed to Luther, it first appeared in *Geistliche Lieder, auffs new gebessert zu Wittenberg. Dr. Martin Luther, 1529.*

trade in the eleventh century, merchant classes and guilds developed which came into conflict with the secular powers. Various interested parties could join forces at different times and in different combinations in order to change the dominance of a section of the community. When the town party was victorious, the castle was destroyed because it symbolized the power of the nobility.[1] In Lombardy, the nobles were forced to live in the towns where, however, they allied themselves with the merchant bankers. As power groups changed in character with success or power, the most dominant political forces allied with the despots so that the mass of 'have-nots' would be assured of less likelihood of a voice in affairs. The dominants in a mediaeval town were all expressive of the power of the politically superior forces: the church above all, the Town Hall, the Guild houses and the market place formed the nucleus of a town which was surrounded by walls and may have had a castle as well. The church and castle were the most significant architectural dominants, although in Flanders and in Holland in later times the Town Halls and Guildhalls dominated the town, as in Bruges and Ypres.

Franz Kafka, in 'The Castle,' a symbolic novel,[2] discusses the visible trappings of power and how they affect mankind in an extreme way. The Castle, for K., the nameless figure in the story, is first seen hidden in mist: mysterious and inscrutable. The sense of impotence which grips him in the face of an impenetrable bureaucracy and masses of red tape could not have been the central theme of a novel unless the castle in history had become the oppressor instead of the protector. The Castle thus symbolized what it was, namely power.

The churches and castles were undoubtedly impressive, and in churches especially, symbols were everywhere in evidence. The great towers and spires, symbols of strength and aspirations to the heavens, could be seen from all over the town and from the distant country. Spires and towers today may be seen framed in narrow streets even in what appear to be rambling town plans. A less politically dominant force would not have been so consciously expressed in building.

---

[1] This concept is also mentioned by Aristotle in *Politics* Bk. VII 1330b. p. 206. 'An acropolis is suited to an oligarchy or monarchy, but a level site to democracy.'
[2] *The Castle*, originally *Das Schloss*.

The mediaeval period produced its own city-states, which were political units with town-councils, guild bodies, special liberties for its citizens; and its customs and laws were distinct from those of the country districts which had their roots in feudalism. Eventually, through conflict with the feudal lords and the growth of municipal power through trade, the towns gained more control over the rural areas and a two-way traffic was assured of market produce coming into the towns and the work of craftsmen going out. In addition, the peasantry could count on the protection of the town walls in times of unrest.[1]

Another type of town emerged as the Middle Ages progressed: namely the specialized university town which proliferated in Germany, possibly due to the disruption of the larger political units into small diverse independent states. These towns possess characters all their own, with unique inscapes evoked by the colleges of Oxford and Cambridge, and the townscape of Tübingen.

EXPANSION AND COLONIES

The Eastern Roman Empire maintained its authority in the west through the exarchate of Ravenna, but by the eighth century, due to the incursions of Islam, this authority was crumbling. In addition, the iconoclastic movement induced a schism between the western and eastern Churches. Spain had mostly fallen to Islam, and the Muslims had their capital in the magnificent and enlightened city of Cordoba where all faiths were tolerated, and a cultured community dwelt in peace. The Empire was hard pressed in the east, and the Papacy found itself without a secular protector. The Pope needed the Franks to guarantee his position, so after Pope Leo III had visited Charles, King of the Franks, at Paderborn, the king subsequently visiting Rome, was crowned *Imperator Augustus* in A.D. 800.

This coronation was an illegal act, for the Pope had no power to create an emperor, yet from this event was born the Holy Roman Empire which lasted until 1806. It was called the *Roman Empire* from 1034, and the term *Roman Emperor* was used to describe its head from the reign of Otto II (died A.D. 983).

The Papacy regarded the Empire as the secular arm of the Church. The imperial theorists saw its function as that of conquest

---

[1] *The West European City*, Chapter 14, gives a well detailed account of the nature of types of mediaeval settlement.

and hegemony from which it drew its power and the emperor as being responsible to God alone. The popular theory, meaning that of the influential ruling classes, was that the Empire was a continuance of the delegation of power by the Roman patricians.

In A.D. 812 Constantinople recognized the imperial title, though as *Emperor*, not *Roman Emperor*. The consequence of this was a rivalry which culminated in the disaster of 1204, when the 'Latin Empire' was established in Constantinople.

After the reign of Louis the Pious, the Carolingian Empire dissolved, but the Saxon King Henry I was acclaimed emperor after A.D. 933, and his son, Otto I, who became king of the Eastern Franks in A.D. 936, was crowned by Pope John XII in A.D. 962. Otto did not claim dominion over the West Franks, and after his reign the *Empire* meant Germany and northern Italy. Otto II (A.D. 973–983) became *Roman Emperor*, and the Empire itself became the *Roman Empire* in the reign of Conrad II (A.D. 1024–1039). The Papacy became subordinated to the emperor during the reign of Otto III (A.D. 983–1002) and from A.D. 962–1046, the emperor was looked on as God's vicar on earth rather than the Pope. The power and supremacy of the politico-religious emperors are symbolized in the mighty cathedrals of Speyer and Worms, colossal dominants in the strong, self confident German Romanesque style. Eight emperors are buried in Speyer, and in the great cathedral of Worms lies Kaiser Conrad II.

When the Normans overran southern Italy and Sicily, they bolstered up the Papacy against the Empire for their own ends. The Norman invasion of England produced a monumental style of architecture in both churches and castles. Castle Hedingham, Winchester, Durham and Ely Cathedrals are all expressive of the strength of will and stability brought by William the Norman in his ruthless policy of subduing Saxon England. Contrast a dominant, such as the tower of Earl's Barton Church, Northamptonshire, which has a charming woolly-minded whimsey, with the gigantic power of Durham Cathedral, and the expansionist, domineering character of Norman ambition is expressed.

The Empire became the *Holy Roman Empire* under Frederick Barbarossa. The Hohenstaufen dynasty emphasized the secular foundation of the Empire, despite the title, and the power of their race may be seen at Castel del Monte, Lucera and Palermo, where Barbarossa is buried. It was the Hohenstaufens who give us another hint of that strange yearning for the south which we have already noted. They merge with myth and become Romantic figures from a dimly discerned past: Manfred, Frederick, Roger and Conradin, living their lives in the exotic south, and now only a name or two and a few ruins are there to remind us of that Germanic rule in the southern lands. Even Manfredonia has slumbered now for centuries.

In the west, the chief towns of the Empire had their origins in bishoprics or secular fortresses founded in *castra* or on older settlements, and the most important of these lay near the Rhine and along the great trade routes. The urban cluster grouped itself around the nucleus of church and fortress. The central position of the church in the urban structure was all-important, for the towers, shadows and bulk of the ecclesiastical buildings dominated the town and the relationship between the size of the church and that of the houses that clustered round it is symbolic of the dominant position of the Church as central focus of life and the town.

Dr. Rosenau suggests[1] that the most significant motif recurring in mediaeval towns, which give them a sense of order and homogeneity, was the orientation of the religious buildings. As foci were emphasized architecturally, so they contrasted with the smaller development, and the most important buildings were singled out for dominant treatment. Architectural foci symbolized the dominant influences of Church, municipality, secular power, guilds, and later, of merchants and bankers.

Within the church building were symbols in paintings and sculpture. Augustine's message of the City of God which pervaded Byzantine symbolism, was shown graphically, and the City of God is identified with Jerusalem, a vision that created a potent image for the first Crusades. Dr. Rosenau points out[2] that in many examples of graphic imagery the celestial city is shown as a circular form. This mandala idea is a concept of unity and perfection, and we have encountered this notion in previous chapters. The circular form is developed in the plans of Byzantine churches, while in the west, Theodoric's tomb is octagonal, and the church of St. Costanza is circular. In Constantinople, the great circular dome of Hagia Sophia was a dominant symbol, and in St. Vitale at Ravenna an octagon with a circular dome forms the body of the church. It is to Aachen, however, that we must turn, for the cathedral built by Charles the Great, with its central octagon and great high dark domed interior possesses a crown of light, or *corona*, suspended from

[1]   *The Ideal City* p. 31.
[2]   *Ibid.* p. 26.

the dome. This *corona*, an immense copper gilt candelabrum, was made by Wibert of Aachen, by order of Frederick Barbarossa. Wagner must have had Aachen in mind when he wrote the stage directions for *Parsifal*, for the Hall of the Grail in Wagner's production is based on a very similar form. The Holy Grail, another remarkably potent mediaeval idea, was symbolized as the Chalice, but it is Wagner again who tells us that there is no way to it, and no one knows what it is unless the Grail itself leads 'der reine Tor' to it. The Grail, in such a setting, becomes the centre of a mandala form and is surrounded by a corona of light, but when the Grail is uncovered, itself emits a radiant light. The mandala form of Aachen Cathedral became the centre of a city, the place of coronation and burial of the Carolingian emperors, and the centre of the Empire, and was therefore a symbol itself, and a major architectural dominant.

From the beginning of the Middle Ages a regular type of plan developed at the same time as the cluster pattern, and this regularity preceded both the time of colonization and the growth of capitalism. This may have been due to the existence of regular Roman prototypes, but there may also have been cosmological significance in such plans, as well as the obvious advantages of easy sub-division.

The main elements of the mediaeval town plan were the centre: with church, Town Hall, Guild buildings, inns and market square; and the wall which defined the town and separated it from the country, making it an island.[1] The walls in a way symbolized the inviolability of the mediaeval city, and when the first guns battered the walls down, the outer symbol of the mediaeval urban ethos lost its validity, and mediaeval society was doomed with it.

The market place and church together formed what might be likened to agora and acropolis, the profane and the sacred, united in the urban nucleus. The inscape of the mediaeval town is directly related to the humanity of this wholeness and to its sympathetic scale. Many markets were originally founded by cloistered orders under a permission granted by Kaiser Otto II (973–983). The monasteries existed as havens from all the uncertain factors outside, as well as keeping the spark of learning alight. The Benedictines, in addition to preserving Roman techniques, were practitioners of building, painting and the design and manufacture of stained glass, but, more than anything, they preserved the written record.

[1] *The Culture of Cities* p. 53.

According to Hegel, in the tenth century most of the market foundations were given to the Church rather than to the towns, and thus the orders and bishoprics grew rich.

Under Kaisers Henry and Otto the Great (933–973) a vast defence system was developed to counter the raids of northmen. Otto established many bishoprics on the Elbe, and he strengthened the defences of Aachen, Mainz, Worms, Trier and Magdeburg. The consolidation of the Empire in the west was followed by the colonization movement east, which began under Otto the Great.

New towns were constructed for defence purposes and for colonization, and the Empire expanded into the Prussian plains, into the valleys of Thuringia, along the Baltic and far into the eastern marks. These centres had a new character, a formality, and the number of Neustadts speaks for itself as to the enormous movement of colonization. It was from the enlightened historical imaginations of Kaisers Otto the Great and Conrad II (1024–1039) that the German urbanization movement grew, as defences against the Slavs and as trading centres. Mumford estimates the number of new towns in the eastern marks over four centuries as 2500,[1] while Hoehn is more conservative, putting the figure at 2000 between the years 900 and 1400, although he includes in his estimates those older foundations which were raised to the status of town by imperial charter.[2]

The wave of colonization in the east, beyond the Elbe and its bishoprics which had been previously established by Otto I, came to an end in the fourteenth century, by which time German influences had penetrated far east, into Pomerania and beyond. To encourage trade in the Baltic, Lübeck was reconstructed in 1143 and cities were established at intervals along the Baltic shore. The Lübeck plan became the model for these colonial settlements, and not only its plan but its architectural style as well. Lübeck, once a great Hanseatic port has, even today, an inscape of great power. The Marienkirche dominates the town, and the Rathaus, strangely, evokes Venetian images, demonstrating the influence of commercial enterprise and travel on the design of towns within the Zeitgeist of the time. The connection with Venice, based on the trade routes, is also strengthened when we recall that Lübeck is famous for marzipan, or St. Mark's bread. The imageability of Lübeck as it is

---

[1] *The Culture of Cities* p. 23.
[2] *History Builds the Town* p. 48.

approached from the Baltic is unforgettable, demonstrating in the predominance of spires the power of the Church, and making one aware that the design of the town as a three-dimensional problem, both inside it and beyond it, was fully understood by the mediaeval planners.

The Hanseatic towns were modelled on Lübeck, which was the head of the League, and all had similar functions. A regular planned basic form is apparent, with rectangular sites left for churches, the market and the civic centre, although the walls varied with the topography and size of the town, and thus had similarities with Greek forerunners. The market places had central positions, but had good access to the harbours. All the Hanseatic towns had high gabled houses of the merchants and bankers, and an extraordinary architecture of red-brick Gothic developed, giving a peculiar character to them.

The term *bastide* originally meant a fortress, but it is as a term for a colonial town with which we are concerned. Just as once forts had been built to defend settlements against barbarian attack, so *bastides* developed originally as fortified areas attached to monasteries. In France, new towns were built by Louis IX after he had conquered the Albigensian heretics. The new towns he established were built for military reasons, to consolidate his own rule. These *bastides* were models for those of Edward I of England, who decided on the building of fortified towns to form nuclei for the furtherance and maintenance of his own power in France and in Wales.

Bastides were laid out on a regular plan, and were obviously planned consciously. Cecil Stewart[1] tells us that after the site had been selected, the boundary of the town would be established, and this was usually a rectangle. Walls would be built by the founder, and the plots would be laid out on the regular pattern of the Roman *insulae*. Central rectangles were kept for the market, town hall and church, which itself might be fortified. Dr. Rosenau states[2] that it was the individual unit and not the whole city which was planned.

Settlers were encouraged to live in the *bastides* by special conditions, such as the gift of land, plots for building and tax relief, but in return, the buildings had to be up within a certain time, and conform with certain standards.[3] This was not so difficult, as the

[1] *A Prospect of Cities* pp. 80–81.
[2] *The Ideal City* p. 30.
[3] *A Prospect of Cities* p. 81.

manners of design and the techniques of craftsmanship aided the uniformity of the appearance of the towns. Squares were often arcaded and perfect squares. The *bastides* are laid out clearly and logically, and were designed to be built at one time and remain like that, as indeed many of them have remained.

Louis IX (1226–1270) built Carcasonne and Aigues Mortes, which was an assembly point for the Crusades,[1] but Edward I, Louis' nephew, was responsible for many more, including Montpazier, Villeneuve-sur-Lot and St. Foy-la-Grande. Aigues Mortes is thus a town which developed in importance purely because of the symbolism of the celestial city, for the Crusades were aimed at freeing the Holy Land, and especially Jerusalem, City of God, from Islam. It has been estimated that over 200 new towns were built in France in the thirteenth century, but only a few matured into real towns. Many failed, and some just stopped growing, like Mont-

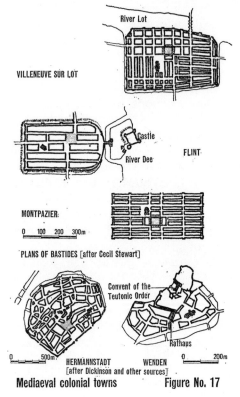

PLANS OF BASTIDES [after Cecil Stewart]

Mediaeval colonial towns   Figure No. 17

[after Dickinson and other sources]

---

[1]   *History Builds the Town* p. 48.

pazier. Conceived as entities, they remained static. We have seen how the removal of the walls by cannon symbolized the end of the mediaeval city. The opposite is true, in that Aigues Mortes and Montpazier which are preserved intact, with walls, retained the physical form of the Middle Ages, but they ceased to be important because they became fossils of another period.

War with the Welsh in 1276 forced Edward to establish *bastides* at Flint, Conway, Harlech and other points, and the English were encouraged to settle there. They also acted as bases from which the English armies could subdue the Welsh. The plan of Flint, with its regular streets, fortified ditches and great castle to the north, expresses its military origins, just as the French *bastides* conjure up visions of modified Roman fortified towns. In contrast, the German colonial towns, which were founded in largely virgin territory to resist Slav invasions, seem more organically connected with the various peaceful functions of towns, and consequently are further away from the Roman *castrum* in development than the English and French *bastides*. Indeed, ease of troop movements within the town was a feature of the *bastide* layout.

As trade revived in the eleventh century, so a general revitalization of the west commenced, and a new collective sense of security developed, enhanced by the existence of walled fortress-towns and by the new political stability. A combination of these factors brought about the re-opening of the great trade routes, and so settlements, from Constantinople to Venice, thence to Augsburg and overland to the Rhine, then down to Flanders and the Baltic Sea, grew rich and prosperous. Fairs were established at various centres, and these were the foundations of the growth of the great capitalist cities. Fairs and trade encouraged the exchange of ideas, and the spread of cultural heritage and fashionable modes alike.

It is often forgotten that, in addition to the Church, the master-craftsmen handed down from generation to generation a considerable part of the European heritage. Hans Sachs is a good example of the master-craftsman, philosopher, poet and musician, and it is significant that Wagner, who sought a synthesis of the arts in his *Gesamtkunstwerk*, should have created such a sympathetic figure in his own Hans Sachs in *Die Meistersinger von Nürnberg*. Pogner himself says:

'. . . wir im weiten deutschen Reich
Die Kunst einzig noch pflegen . . .'[1]

[1] in the German Empire, only we (the Masters) still cherish Art.

The inscape of the mediaeval town suggests at once the calm and closely knit social organism of a great self-sufficient society, confident yet humble, proud of its traditions, yet paying devotion to a something beyond, real, and part of the experience of everyday life. Anyone who has felt the inscape of Rothenburg-ob-der-Tauber, Landsberg-am-Lech, Solbad Hall or Stein-Krems cannot escape the sense of rightness, humility and yet tremendous sureness of touch that inspired the builders. Apart from the human scale of the buildings and plans, there are, on all sides reminders of the spiritual quality in mediaeval life, not least in Rothenburg, whose church possesses a magnificent altarpiece by Tilman Riemenschneider.

Venice became a thriving city in the tenth century, and by the eleventh, it was a great sea-power. Under Frederick Barbarossa, a modern centralized power-state emerged, which exercised dominion over everything, including culture. The trade monopoly which the Hohenstaufen reserved was backed up by a secret police and a harsh system of taxation.[1] Upper Italian towns had to pay huge revenues to the emperor, but in exchange enjoyed self-government, and it is from this period, the twelfth century, that Milan, Florence, Pisa, Genoa and Venice grew to positions of supremacy in the west, with a bias towards republican forms of government, although these tended to be governments of ruling classes of merchant bankers and capitalist princes.

Florence seems to have derived its aesthetic qualities from the awareness of its ruling classes, and should be regarded as a product of civic pride which was expressible due to the success of Florentine trading activities.

THE FINAL PHASE

If the towns of Lombardy and Venetia concentrated on trade and sea-power, the late Middle Ages saw the rise of the towns of Flanders, the Hanseatic League, and the capitals of the nation-states. The cloth industry was centred on Bruges, Ghent, Malines and Ypres, and English wool was the raw material. Commercial intercourse and banking activities centred on London; Lombardy and Flanders thrived, and international trade developed as the products of the weavers travelled all over Europe. Flanders, with its concentration of weavers, became strongly urbanized by the thirteenth century, and prospered greatly.

[1] *Reflections on History* p. 82.

The Hanse developed as the towns banded into a league for mutual protection of interests controlling the trade in the Baltic Sea. The Hanse had ramifications in Russia as well as in Scandinavia, and had the monopoly of northern dealings in furs, wax, skins, timber, grain and copper. At the height of its power it included nearly 80 towns,[1] and the architectural dominants express the homogeneity of that power. With the rise of nations, however, the free cities declined, and when trade passed from the inland seas to the great oceans, the power and money passed on too. The Hanseatic towns and their Italian counterparts became less important than the cities which developed with outlets nearer the Atlantic coast. The discovery of America completed this process.

Paris grew in importance as a seat of the monarchy, the Church and the university, which was the most famous in Europe. But it was established in a position of unique power by the fact that France emerged as one of the first nation-states which gave Europe the new secular order. The monarchy had originally had its seat in the city, in the urban nucleus with the cathedral. However, in the twelfth and thirteenth centuries, the Louvre fortress was built *outside* the city, symbolizing the sundering of the monarchy from the social organism. Even Sainte Chapelle had a degree of richness unparalleled in Europe, not for its religious significance, but because it was the shrine of King Louis IX.

In the Netherlands, where a struggle with the elements was the essence of existence, it is interesting to note that the Dutch succeeded, by mastery of techniques of engineering, in creating a society based on urban centres and reclaimed land in which dominants do not occur in the same sense as in other countries. Harmonious cities were built by canals and the fusing of individual lives with communities is expressed by the homogeneity and simple charm of the Dutch towns and cities. By the end of the mediaeval period, unlike other countries, the majority of Dutchmen were living in cities. The conditions of the soil were such that often the first communal buildings of any importance were the water offices which were responsible for the maintenance of a constant level in canals.

In Delft, the typical Dutch town is symbolized, with canals, roads, bridges and houses forming units in a whole. Dutch cities tend to be very compact for the simple reasons that land is scarce,

[1] *History Builds the Town* p. 50.

and piling was necessary, so costs could be kept down by carrying the weight on a cross-wall construction. The qualities of light found in the interiors of houses painted by Vermeer were possible because of this type of construction.[1] The centre of Delft is the market square which is bounded by houses with stepped gables. Facing each other, across the square are the Nieuwe Kerk of 1381, where the mausoleum of the House of Orange-Nassau is situated; and the Raadhuis of 1520. The main canal, the Oude Delft canal is terminated visually by the Oude Kerk of 1250, yet somehow these churches are not dominants in the same way as in Germany, France, England or Italy, probably because the civic buildings are strongly expressed. A civilized atmosphere pervades Dutch cities, which possess inscapes of great charm.

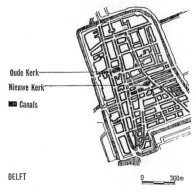

Oude Kerk
Nieuwe Kerk
■ Canals

DELFT   0 ____ 300m

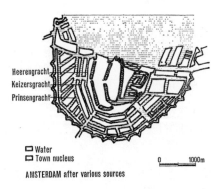

Heerengracht
Keizersgracht
Prinsengracht

☐ Water
☐ Town nucleus   0 ____ 1000m
AMSTERDAM after various sources

Dutch towns   Figure No. 18

[1]   *Towns and Buildings* p. 81.

Amsterdam became a symbol of the Dutch political climate, for here a unity pervades the city. Amsterdam grew by simply digging another canal beyond the original, and placing a new line of fortifications within. This process went on, until the characteristic plan developed as a series of ring canals. Significantly, Dutch democracy is expressed in the names, for the first canal near the core is the Heerengracht, then comes the Keizersgracht, and finally, the Prinsengracht. Walking or boating in Amsterdam, one is struck by the architectural and civic tradition, with a lack of overbearing dominants. Occasionally, a tower is seen and vistas are stopped by towers which usually turn out to be of a municipal origin, for minting, water or defence. The churches are played down, and wallow like great brick amiable animals in the urban matrix of brothels and pubs. Although Amsterdam developed mostly from the end of the sixteenth century, it has been mentioned in this chapter because of the mediaeval core and the fact that the form of development had already started in the Middle Ages. Tradition and modernity join, as in Switzerland, and uncomfortable changes of style are not so much in evidence as, say, in England.

After the sixteenth century, many mediaeval towns lost the dynamism which might have carried them on to develop. The better the walls were preserved, the more this expressed the decline in importance of the city. We have seen how the mediaeval town grew, and how it had distinguished itself from the countryside, but changing methods of warfare, and changing attitudes to rural life had lessened the distinction. Towns were no longer safe, and, with the growth of the fashionable panegyric on the charms of country life foreshadowing the Arcadian movement of the eighteenth century, people now chose to live in rural areas without the social stigma of being considered either serfs or peasants. The rise of nation-states hastened the decline of cities, and at the same time brought about political security in the country. With the decline of towns, so their institutions grew feeble, as towns are social phenomena. Now industry could flourish in the no longer barbarous countryside, and so work could be farmed out to the cottage industries at cheaper rates than the Guilds laid down. The Guilds had established monopolies, but they were based on mutual effort and benefit, sited in towns and under the control of responsible bodies. In the sixteenth century, however, the new monopolies were vested in individuals, and it is from this time that ruthless capitalism developed on a really modern scale as the old order collapsed.

Money bought titles, land, power and lives, just as it has always done. Even the Church was taken over by the head of the nation-state in England, and its papal throne was occupied by members of the great merchant banker families.

The mediaeval *status quo* was challenged often enough, but apart from the Swabian League, the Hanseatic League and the Flemish cities, it was never successfully displaced by unions of city-states. When the municipalities threw their lot in with the kings in order to overthrow localized power, they emerged afterwards less free than they had been previously, as each move consolidated the power of the nation-state. A loose federation of cities within the framework of the Holy Roman Empire worked for a while, but when the Empire itself became the subject of power struggles between Spain, France, Germany and Austria, and was torn apart by religious strife, the system collapsed. Only in the Netherlands and in Switzerland was there a unity formed between the towns and the country, and both had highly democratic traditions.

The nation-states developed rapidly in England and France, as the dynastic struggles ended in England, and France emerged united after the Hundred Years' War. Compared with the fragmented Empire, where tolls and barriers existed at every frontier, the economic advantage passed immediately to France and England.

The Church had become corrupted in this period, and the values of material possessions replaced those of the spirit. The corruption of the Church was manifest, as even the indulgence was given for hard cash. Yet religion had been a part of the life of the people, and it had given the *raison d'être* to many towns and cities, as well as providing nuclei and foci for urban development. By the end of the mediaeval period it had become polytheistic with the growth of such cults as the *Nothelfer*,[1] the Virgin and the patrons of cities. The latter recalls the city gods of ancient civilizations, and might be described as neo-paganism. Popular legends of Tales of the Virgin permeated daily life and art. A vital religion is hand in hand with a culture, and it occupied the imaginations of men to a considerable degree in those days. The Black Death of the fourteenth century was responsible for much. The light of the Renaissance as an intellectual force had begun to shine in the time of Dante and Giotto, but the plague arrested the development, causing social and political chaos;

[1] Helpers in need.

the rise of military despotism to restore order; and the suppression of intellectual freedom, something which invariably happens in time of emergency. From those dark days came superstition, reaction and fear. In the enlightened days of Charles the Great, Otto I and Conrad II, belief in witchcraft had been rejected, but the Church sanctioned it in 1484, thus causing the ghastly persecution of the unpopular and the insane which was to build up to the mass burnings and torturings of the sixteenth and seventeenth centuries. The ruthlessness of the capitalist princes and the frightfulness of the contemporary popes coincided with this period, and wholesale hysteria developed in the Dominican and popular imaginations until it might seem that Beelzebub himself had taken over.

After Luther, in 1521, said *Hier stehe ich, ich kann nicht anders,*[1] Christianity re-established salvation as an inner process, and the finding of grace in faith. Unfortunately, the purified atmosphere of Protestantism threw all the old symbols out, and the quality of the purity was symbolized in the bare churches which left all to the imagination. Now the Protestant had to conjure up his own images, which might, human nature being what it is, turn out to be anything but pure. The Counter-Reformation for this reason ran riot with imagery, pomp and symbols in its churches, to restore forcibly the bond with popular imagery, hence the art of the baroque period.

Protestantism became nationalistic in character, and as differences in dogma sundered the Empire, so the sense of community in the cities declined. The physical town became shabby, for its institutional buildings no longer housed institutions with functions, yet some mediaeval institutions were revitalized, such as monasticism, which, in the Society of Jesus became militant.

As the old order died, so did its symbols, and with the rise of a new society, so new dominants appeared. The monumental road, the buildings of commerce and power, the princely churches and, above all, the palaces, show us that the world of Hans Sachs had vanished to be replaced by a new one, to culminate in that of *Le Roi Soleil.*

[1] 'Here I stand, I cannot do otherwise.'

VI

The Renaissance

INTRODUCTION

We have seen, briefly, how the civilization of the Middle Ages came to an end to be replaced by something quite different. With the end of feudalism was born the nation-state. The leisurely building of the great mediaeval cathedrals suddenly stopped, leaving truncated unfinished towers, incomplete naves and spireless silhouettes all over Europe, symbolic perhaps of the slackening power of the Church. New dominants began to appear, new ruling classes, and above all, a new Zeitgeist pervaded the west.

The animosity between the Hohenstaufen and the papacy created a political climate in Italy which differed from other western regions. In Spain (where the Islamic civilization had been destroyed), France and England, the feudal system assisted the formation of new nations, but in Italy a multiplicity of political units existed which neither Empire nor papacy could control. Thomas Aquinas had discussed theories of constitutional monarchy, but in a country where despots and brigand-princes ruled with dictatorial powers in their own cities, such wishful thinking just was incapable of implementation in reality. The tyrants in the Italy of the fourteenth century beggar description, and they did not improve with the next. These dynasties placed themselves above the law, and legitimate and illegitimate offspring were liberally bestowed with goods and power, so that they fought among themselves for supremacy with a ferocity which stained the pages of Italian history with oceans of blood.

Emperors came and went, usually to sell privileges for money, and the tyrants remained in power, usually with a few more titles to add to their prestige. Under Kaiser Maximilian I, however, a new policy developed, namely imperial intervention in Italian affairs. Under Charles V, the Empire was unified with a strong leadership, and, with Spanish forces, it was able to re-assert its authority to back the papacy. This intervention caused the Papal

States to be regarded as puppet-states of foreign powers, since Charles V was first of all king of Spain, and secondly Holy Roman Emperor.

The rise of Spain coincides with the shift of power as trade developed from the inland seas to the great intercontinental routes. The sudden influx of gold looted from the unfortunate civilizations of America which increased the wealth of Spain, widened her markets, increased her production and made her a dominant European power, also called into being large standing armies and fleets. These latter became accepted attributes of power and the prerogatives of kings, and the new-found might of Spain was added to the power of the Empire, whose head was the king of Spain. With the growth of such mighty secular power and the decline of the Church, the new political dominants demanded new symbols: great luxuries and noble residences.

In Italy too, from the mid-fourteenth century, came a new cult: that of the birthplaces, houses and places of burial of famous men. Petrarch was so honoured, and the cell of Thomas Aquinas was also revered.[1] Prior to this change of custom, pilgrimages had been made to pictures and relics, but in fourteenth century Florence, the monuments of Accorso, Dante, Boccaccio, Petrarch, della Strada and others were ornamented and revered, although often, as in the case of Dante, the corpse was elsewhere. From this time also grew the cult of remembering famous men of the past. Burckhardt, in *The Civilization of the Renaissance in Italy* Part II, draws our attention to the rise of the importance of the individual in Renaissance culture. The new Zeitgeist exalted individual men above the collective achievement of the previous epoch.

The Renaissance commenced in Italy with the proximity of antique remains a powerful stimulus. It must not be forgotten that classicism had never really died in Italy, for even the Gothic movement had little impact except in the north which was very much bound with the fortunes of the Empire and its Germanic spirit. In a sense, then, Italy returned to her vernacular motifs in the renaissance period.

As the new Zeitgeist spread, so it became the credo of all the intelligentsia of Europe. At the same time its very nature, that of being so much involved with classical literature and philosophy, made it an upper-class movement, and so sharply separated the

[1] *The Civilization of the Renaissance in Italy* p. 77.

learned and unlearned classes. This new self-conscious movement differed from earlier periods, such as the Carolingian age which produced great architectural monuments with more than a hint of antique prototypes. The Romanesque architecture of the Empire and the Frankish kingdoms of the north also possessed remarkable allusions to classical forms, probably owing to the influence of the monasteries which had preserved so much antique technique. Yet in Italy itself, where so much of classical culture was a part of everyday life, and even the language was so much akin to Italian, all classes were equally involved, and such a schism between classes was avoided. In literature, too, much Italian poetry had been influenced by Latin predecessors, and even in the *Carmina Burana* of the twelfth century, pagan imagery appears. It will hardly be necessary to mention Virgil and Dante together as a reminder.

The fourteenth and fifteenth centuries saw a tremendous revival of interest in the ruins of ancient Rome which in those days were in a good state of preservation. Descriptions by Poggio and others tell us of a pastoral Rome, where peasants kept their livestock among the ruins of the Forum and on the slopes of the Capitol. Unfortunately, thousands of marble columns and carvings must have perished in that period, since marble is easily burnt into quicklime.

With the election of Pope Nicholas V in the mid-fifteenth century, the papacy came into the forefront of the renaissance urge to study antiquities and build after the fashion of the ancients. These activities were both dangerous as well as beneficial to the ruins, for they could be pillaged for materials or swept away for new development. The discoveries of ancient murals, statues, such as the Apollo Belvedere, the Laocoön, the Vatican Venus, and other antique remains excited the renaissance imagination, and gave new stimuli to creation as well as to collection. Ancient books and papers were rediscovered and copied, and the classics were read again with enthusiasm and excitement. Printing multiplied the availability of the ancient authors to a wider intelligentsia. Another factor, of course, in the revival of learning in the classics, was the influx of large numbers of Greek scholars after the fall of Constantinople to the Turks. When Greece itself became Turkish, Hellenic culture seemed even more unbearably nostalgic and irretrievable.

The rise of humanism, too, dates from the time of Boccaccio, who argued that paganism could be studied with safety now that true religion was everywhere established. A Platonic Academy was established in Florence, one of its central studies being the reconciliation of the classic spirit with Christianity. Paganism, however, brought influences which were decidedly unhealthy, for the growth of superstition coincides with the revival of interest in antiquity. Astrology became respectable, and from the fourteenth to the sixteenth century universities had professors in astrology, while princes, rich despots and free cities had their own resident astrologers. The popes, too, turned to astrology, and it seems to have exercised a paralysing effect on public life. Journeys, receptions and even the laying of foundation stones were subject to the rulings of the astrologers. Burckhardt[1] tells us that the city walls at Forlì were rebuilt under a constellation indicated by the astrologer Bonatto.

From the fourteenth century onwards, belief in witchcraft, demons, ghosts, ghouls and other disagreeable phantoms seems to have spread, aided and abetted by astrology and by the chaos and dark night of the Black Death. Legends of the Mount of Venus proliferated, where magical arts were taught, and all manner of amorous joys were practised. In 1484, the bull of Innocent VIII gave the official seal and recognition to the existence of witchcraft, and all hell was thereafter let loose. Images of horror appeared in the forms of rotting corpses, demons and vile creatures in the paintings of Parentino, Carpaccio, Alunno, and witches and alchemists were portrayed by Botticelli, Stradano and others.

The portraits of tyrants, princes and popes of the period give us some insight as to the rise of an utterly ruthless and materialist class, nevertheless given to superstition, astrological belief and revolting cruelty. Bentivoglio, Este of Ferrara, Sforza, Gonzaga, Montefeltro, Colleoni, Vitelli, Fondolo, Borgia . . . what a horrifying gallery of faces and names! If the tyrants were shockers, they were secular ones, but the greatest horrors of all were the renaissance popes. The terrible Sixtus IV, who by simony on a vast scale, entrenched himself in a position of great wealth and power, and made the Papal States a political force again. Nepotism was rampant, and papal offspring were given powerful sinecures in the Church. Innocent VIII, who succeeded Sixtus, publicly acknowledged his children, one of his sons marrying a daughter of Lorenzo the Magnificent. Secular pardons were sold for huge sums, and the papal families grew richer and richer, and consequently more powerful. On one occasion a whole embassy of Maximilian's court from Innsbruck was stripped, robbed and sent back without being allowed access to Rome at all.

[1] *The Civilization of the Renaissance in Italy* p. 270.

Pope Alexander VI and his vile son Caesar ruled the Papal States with a terror machine. So great were their crimes and their lust for secular power that the greatest danger for the papacy in those days was the personality of the Pope. Paradoxically, it was Caesar Borgia who was looked on by some as a possible saviour of Italy, for by destroying the papacy the source of all foreign intervention would have been removed and Italy would have united. The Papal States were always backed by foreign Roman Catholic powers, and it was not until the nineteenth century and Garibaldi with the creation of the Kingdom of Italy that the Papal States ceased to exist.

There can be no doubt that the Crusades gave new horizons to European minds. Marco Polo, from Venice, had ventured far into the Mongolian lands, and brought back tales of the wonders of Cathay. Christopher Columbus was one of many Italian voyagers who sailed into uncharted seas, and his discoveries opened up new lands for European adventurers. The urban civilization of America astonished the conquerors, especially the Aztec capital of Tenochtitlan which was captured by Cortes in 1519. This seat of a militarist theocracy was divided into four parts, four being a magic number. It was situated in the middle of a lake and served by an aqueduct and by causeways. Its dominants were the enormous temples on stepped ziggurat-like bases where the gods were appeased with great numbers of human sacrifices. To the Spaniards, Tenochtitlan was impressive, not only because of its population which was around 80,000, but because of the architectural splendours of temples and palaces. The subjection of the American empires, however, provided a new source of wealth for the European powers. Spain and Portugal certainly built up their bullion in this period.

There was, of course, another very strong reason for the explorations of the time. After 1453, Turks and Saracens blocked the main trading routes between Europe and Asia. The monopoly of Venice, too, caused western European merchants to think of extending their markets to avoid a Venetian stranglehold on trade. This mercantile and naval power had built itself an incredibly rich city with the profits of trade and its loot in war. The Doge had a splendid palace, and the Piazzo and Cathedral glorified Venetian prowess in art and the collection of wealth. In order to by-pass both Venice and the Turks, explorers discovered new areas for exploitation in Africa, and the Cape route to India was developed in 1486–1498. A Portuguese monopoly of this trade, which even carried them into

China, turned the Spaniards westwards towards India, but they colonized America instead. Bankers of the Hanseatic League helped to finance such expeditions, but the enormous wealth which poured into the maritime states soon helped them to political power far above that of the older trading centres. Flanders became a new centre for banking and trade centred on Antwerp, which was a free city.

The English sought yet another route to India, namely the North-West passage, but colonized Newfoundland in lieu of the trade route. After the House of Orange had defeated the Spaniards in Holland at the end of the sixteenth century, Holland joined the scramble, colonizing parts of America, such as New Amsterdam (now New York), and Surinam, Ceylon, Curaçao, parts of South Africa and the East Indies. Amsterdam itself grew rapidly in the seventeenth century, and Holland became the greatest naval power of the period. The richness of Holland was expressed in the burghers' houses, town halls and guild offices which were built solidly and with good proportions and craftsmanship. The present Royal Palace in Amsterdam was originally the Town Hall.

The design of towns in the Europe of the renaissance period changed slowly at first from the mediaeval spirit. At first, the rise of secularization was expressed by the buildings of individual palaces within the form of the city, such as in Florence. New emphases were placed on values based on the aesthetics of the classical period, since the formality and grandeur of antique design seemed lavish enough to express the ambition and egocentricity of the merchant-princes. This growth of individualism based on the rise of capitalism and the growth of the secular movement is noted by Burckhardt as we have seen.

Rich and powerful men extended their patronage to artists just as once the Church had fulfilled this function. Now, the rediscovery of antique motifs and the revival of portraiture provided new media within which the artists could work. Under the rule of Cosimo de' Medici, Florence produced much of its finest artistic achievements, but with his death in 1492, Savonarola, prior of the Convent of San Marco, sprang into fame. This puritan encouraged the destruction of much Florentine art as well as classical writings, and organized a kind of juvenile moral police who were charged with the collection of objects which were regarded as sinful. Savonarola was hanged and burnt in 1498, but not before he had shown the world a new and dangerous reversion to the destructive mood of puritanism reminiscent of the aura surrounding the sage of Croton.

The anti-beauty, anti-flesh, anti-enjoyment brigade have turned up frequently in the history of human society. In the case of Savonarola and his successors of similar ilk, although many were on the protestant side of the religious fence, there was an explanation for the success of their teaching. In the fifteenth century, a highly virulent form of venereal disease, syphilis, had made its appearance, and caused a great deal of suffering and death. This hideous disease, coming so quickly on the heels of the Black Death, seemed a punishment to many for sexual indulgence. Socially, its appearance put the public baths out of business. In the Middle Ages, public baths were a feature of life, but early in the sixteenth century they disappeared from the urban scene. The spread of syphilis no doubt had something to do with this, and bathing became synonymous with sin and luxurious living, while not bathing became associated with purity, so the odour of sanctity became, one imagines, considerably more pungent.

The magnificent palaces of the Medicis and others in Florence represented a new, rich and secular society, yet the adornments of Florence were superimposed upon a mediaeval city plan. This period was not characterized by vistas and avenues, but might be regarded as one of façadism, when the classical idiom was imposed on the mediaeval street face. Public life took place in the plazas of Italian cities, and these were adorned with splendid statuary and fountains. The functions of forum and market place remained, but the physical spaces were embellished with ornaments which were the products of the artists patronized by the new ruling classes. Public announcements were made in the plaza, and the town hall usually faced the open square. Pisa is an unusual city in that it possesses in its Piazza del Duomo a space of purely religious significance, with Cathedral, Baptistery, *Campo Santo* and Campanile grouped together as a type of religious focus rather like the acropolis of old.[1] This is unusual, however, for squares were usually used for town functions, such as announcements, markets, processions, and burnings of heretics. The square had a basic relationship with the buildings round it, and with the social life of the city.

THE IDEAL CITIES

We have noticed how gunpowder rendered mediaeval fortifications useless. There was a tendency, therefore, for towns to spread once

---

[1]   See *City Planning according to Artistic Principles* pp. 13–19.

the corset was removed, but the spread would not be excessive because of transport limitations. The men of the Renaissance turned their minds to developing new defences for cities, spurred on, no doubt, by the tyrants who were their patrons. Massive new-style fortifications were developed, with earthworks, bastions and artillery-resistant walls, which once more made the fortified city possible and restored a degree of security to its citizens. These new cannon-resistant fortifications were enormously expensive to construct, and consequently, to move. The result was that, as the city grew, terrible overcrowding occurred within its walls. Continental cities thus developed apartment living, while in England the same problem did not arise, due to internal unification, the natural defence of the sea, and a lack of urban tradition.

The new despotisms based on monopoly rapidly grew to tyranny on a national scale, for conditional freedom was the order of the Zeitgeist. The merchant-bankers equipped the monarchs with standing armies to reinforce the stability so necessary for trade. The state replaced the town as the unit for economic existence, and national capitals developed, fortified by the massive defences of the military engineers. Feudal castles were replaced by stately houses of the monarchs and their favourite princelings.

Despots have the power to order cities built as units, as we have seen, but the very nature of despotism is such that organic diversity must be missing in a plan built as a result of the will of a tyrant. The communal efforts of citizens had produced the wonder of the creative harmony of a Nürnberg, Rothenburg or Nördlingen. The complexities of the mediaeval social organism were replaced by a new simplified one in the renaissance period, when new cities began to be regarded as units conceived in the mind of one man, as an entity and as a static unchanging entity at that: the *città ideale*. The rediscovery of Vitruvius and the development of fortifications created this type, which permeated city planning thinking for a long time, and was manifested as a series of designs based on mandala forms. Basically, the *città ideale* consisted of a polygon with fortified walls and a central core. The bastions accentuated the star-shaped design and the formal mandala pattern of the plans.

The centrally organized building occupied the imaginations of Renaissance architects, and the dome returned as an architectural dominant in city design. Similarly, a centrally organized city would express the same central focus. Giedion suggests[1] that the *città ideale*

[1] *Space, Time and Architecture* p. 45.

was a rationalization of a mediaeval city with its central core, which we have discussed in the previous chapter. However, the renaissance designers froze the elements of a city into a formal pattern, with streets which radiated from the centre. I would suggest, however, that there was more to the *città ideale*, and that it may have been an expression of two things: the longing for Utopia, conceived as perfection and remaining as such; and the symbolic creation of a city on which renaissance man imposed his own ideals and heroic dimensions, while accentuating the egocentric nature of the Zeitgeist.

These designs emerged around the middle of the fifteenth century from the imaginations of Alberti, Filarete and Martini, and it is in Alberti that we find designs for fortresses for tyrants, a significant fact considering the political climate of the day. Alberti was keen on conformity, but suggested that undulating streets, rather like meandering rivers, should be built so that a journey through a town would create the illusion that the place was bigger than its factual size. With the rise of individual wealth and the decline in the guilds, however, it soon became apparent that vanity will out, and that the plutocracy would have to have residences magnificent enough for their station. Alberti observed that the nobility should be segregated from the vulgar, and that they should inhabit magnificent houses along avenues of great length.[1]

Filarete worked out a detailed plan in his project for Sforzinda (1460–1464) which, like Vitruvian prototypes, had eight and sixteen as the major segmental divisions, and had a plaza in the centre of the mandala shape. In the centre of the plaza was to be an enormous tower high enough to dominate not only the town, but to overlook the surrounding countryside. It is significant that the town was named after Francesco Sforza, tyrant prince and patron of Filarete.

Martini (1439–1502) developed the *città ideale* plan to incorporate a spiral street running to the top of a hill, not only for ease of traffic up the steep slope, but to foil cannon fire.

In Sforzinda, the *città ideale*, we find the palace has become the most dominant building of the town with the exception of the great watch tower, which is not surprising, while churches are relegated to places of secondary importance. The most unusual feature of Sforzinda was the proposal to erect a House of Virtue and Vice,

---

[1] *A Prospect of Cities* p. 105.

which was to be ten storeys high containing a brothel, lecture rooms and an astrological college at the top.[1]

Michelangelo developed some highly complex bastions for Florence, and the tremendous size of these had a lasting effect on many subsequent fortification designs, many of them not being removed until the nineteenth century. Another famous name, that of Albrecht Dürer, crops up in connection with town planning and fortifications. Some authorities suggest that he may have been influenced by the plan of Tenochtitlan which had only recently been discovered, but Dr. Rosenau suggests that the woodcut plan may resemble Dürer's drawings purely by coincidence and a resemblance of style, since the functions of Dürer's plan and that of Tenochtitlan were different.[2]

Other Utopians, such as Scamozzi and Vasari, planned ideal cities within polygonal fortifications, but on a traditional grid pattern. The regular squares and streets were thoroughly organized by Scamozzi and Vasari, for they 'had the needs of the army constantly in mind.' Mumford states that 'the uniform streets ... had purely a military basis.'[3]

The threat of Turkish invasion was directly responsible for the building of a *città ideale*, that of Palma Nova, the fortress town of Venice, in 1593. The plan was a polygon of nine sides with eighteen radial streets and a central fortified tower recalling Sforzinda. Palma Nova reflects the political climate of its day: the regular patterning, the conventional rules, the geometrical perfection are all there, but so are the disproportionately large fortifications, a source of enormous capital expenditure initially and for upkeep. Palma Nova symbolizes centralization, the problems of external threat, and the growth of specialization, in the form of a standing army, among other things. As society stratified, hereditary principles replaced elective ones. Wars, religious strife and economic competition from the north and west helped to ossify the cities and society of the Mediterranean, and especially in Italy.

Utopias of the renaissance period were generally circular or polygonal mandala forms, but in Germany, the square, another mandala idea, occurs not only in Dürer but in a design actually carried out: that of Freudenstadt in Württemberg. We have already mentioned Dürer's work in connection with Tenochtitlan, but the

---

[1] *The Ideal City* pp. 38–39.
[2] *Ibid.* p. 43
[3] *The Culture of Cities* pp. 95–96.

square turns up again in *Christianopolis* by J. V. Andreae (1619). Freudenstadt was not influenced by Andreae since his work appeared later than the plans for Freudenstadt prepared by Heinrich Schickhardt (1558–1634). Andreae was a scholar and a humanist and his Christianopolis was to be a well fortified square city with 'one market place, but this one of a very high order.'[1] Freudenstadt too had a large market square, but this was unnaturally large, in fact the dominating motif of the town was its enormous empty heart, which is curious, since the town was founded for religious refugees.

Mannheim, at the junction of the Rhine and Neckar, grew in the seventeenth century as a fortress town which was part of a defence system of the Rhenish princes. The fortifications were enormous, as

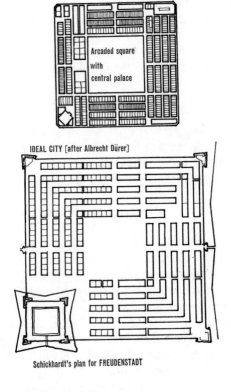

IDEAL CITY [after Albrecht Dürer]

Schickhardt's plan for FREUDENSTADT

Ideal City plans   Figure No. 19

[1] *Urban Development in Central Europe* pp. 307–310.

might be expected of such a strategic position. In the eighteenth century, it became more of a cultural than strategic city, and a palace was erected on the site of the old citadel. Here the musical style of the 'Mannheim School' developed, which was to culminate in the glories of Mozart and Haydn.

THE RISE OF THE NATION-STATES

In the late sixteenth and early seventeenth centuries, unsettled times made defence a major consideration, and more land and capital were consumed by the fortifications. The growth of fortifications and the dominance of military parade grounds and barracks symbolized the new order. The exorbitant expense of standing armies and huge defences made the citizens of towns more and more dependent on the financiers, usually the existing aristocrats, princes or kings. This dependency simply increased the rulers' hold on the towns. These fortifications had become obsolete by the end of the seventeenth century, however, as the military engineers developed the corps of sappers who effectively blew up the most monstrous defences, and with them an intolerable financial burden on the towns.

In Germany, the first half of the seventeenth century was overshadowed by the disasters of the Thirty Years War (1618–1648). It has been estimated that the population of Germany was halved in this time, and the destruction of morale, property and life was truly terrible. The Reformation in Germany had been a popular movement, but the Peasants' War which took things out of the reformers' hands harmed the Reformation because the horrific class hatred displayed in that war made the authorities extra careful that it would not happen again, and so the Reformation movement was 'taken over' by the government. The Hussite troubles became a racial war between Slav and German, and the Counter-Reformation itself became a war between the Protestant nations and the forces of the Empire. In England, Henry VIII, by breaking with Rome and fusing Church and State, changed the future appearance of towns radically. Soon the monasteries had been dissolved, and the secular nobility made rich with church lands. In towns and cities after Henry's death, hundreds of chantry chapels, shrines and monuments were destroyed when prayers for the dead were discontinued. Such a blow at the Church could only have been struck in a climate of growing secularism and rising power of the monarch of a nation-state.

In France the nation-state developed after the expulsion of the English in the fifteenth century and the end of a war which had thinned the ranks of the nobility of both countries. Under King Francis I (1515–1547) Paris grew in splendour, and château building in the Loire valley provided stylish houses for aristocratic courts. Growing markets on an international scale encouraged state production protected by the ruler, and mercantilism or Colbertism developed. The latter, called after Colbert, a minister of Louis XIV, was a theory concerning the part the state had to play in trade, independence and the amassing of capital and power. It involved the formation of a strong national army and navy, a merchant fleet, protection of home industries and the building up of gold reserves. State backed industries developed, as well as state institutes for education. Colonialism grew from this period, and a slave trade, reaching a peak in the eighteenth century, was a foundation upon which labour forces were built in the mines and plantations of the new colonies.

In Germany, Prussia began her rise to power after the Thirty Years War, and immigrants were encouraged to settle in Prussia through fiscal benefits. Industries were backed by the state, and town planning went ahead on a large scale. Berlin had new districts added to it in the late seventeenth century, and the destroyed cities and towns were replanned on a new and splendid scale.

In England, London had long been a city of the first importance, and the City of London had frequently had arguments with both monarch and Church, which it could only have done if it had a unique position in the powerful world of international finance. Prior to the Fire of 1666, London was a typical mediaeval city with walls, churches and a fortress outside (the Tower). West of the City, Inigo Jones had carried out some schemes such as at Covent Garden, for western areas, between the royal city of Westminster and London, became sought after for residential purposes. East of London, the hamlets of Stepney and Hackney formed nuclei for the later spread of residential and working quarters for the poorer citizens. After the Plague and Fire, new regulations came into force to minimize the possibility of future outbreaks of disease and fire. In Wren's plan for the rebuilt City, it is significant that, unlike most European cities, its focus was not a palace or a church, but the Stock Exchange. This plan symbolizes the spirit of London, and expresses its political independence of the state and therefore of the monarchy.

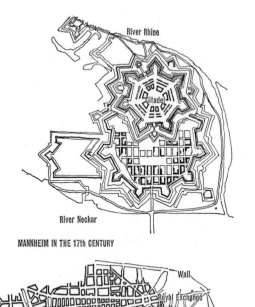

River Rhine

Citadel

River Neckar

MANNHEIM IN THE 17th CENTURY

Wall

Royal Exchange

St Paul's

Tower

River Thames

WREN'S PLAN FOR LONDON 1666

17th century plans   Figure No. 20

At the same time, other developments were taking place in Europe. A new spirit was abroad, and vast palaces were being built for secular princes. The Counter-Reformation had encouraged a tremendous upsurge of church building, and suddenly the world of illusion had been transported from the stage to the Church. Baroque imagery had burst upon the world, and symbolism had come into its own again.

In France, Richelieu and Mazarin had begun the final phase of centralizing power in the hands of the king, a policy which produced the absolute monarchy of *Le Roi Soleil* who symbolized the state.

A ruthless persecution drove the Protestants from France, and the witch-hunt was extended to the liquidation of any dissenting voices. The extraordinary case of the Devils of Loudun and the subsequent torturings of priests and people took place in the period of Richelieu, Corneille, Descartes and Lemercier. We often forget to associate the grand classical scene with such ghastly superstition and hysteria. It was Richelieu who ordered that all buildings round a fortified town should be flattened, and who worked unceasingly for the military greatness of France at the expense of the Empire. He also destroyed the power of the nobles, and concentrated it in the throne. A complete rejection of the past became the quality of the Zeitgeist, and a ruthless destruction of the mediaeval legacy took place, so that buildings in the new taste could be built as stage sets for court parade and ceremonial. In order to show the King how things could be arranged, the Cardinal built the town and château which bear his name. Lemercier designed it, a small, compact walled town, rectangular in plan, with two *places*, a major street and five minor ones. The unity of Richelieu, built as an entity, recalls a

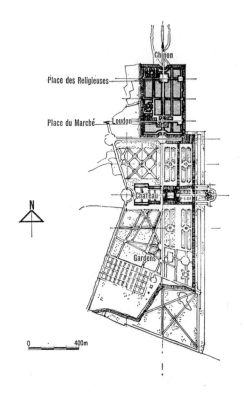

Richelieu: town and château   Figure No. 21

formalized and more sophisticated Roman town in plan, but it also expresses a political climate in which one man, through his architect, could build a total environment, even named after himself.

Richelieu, founded in 1631, is near Chinon and Loudun: perhaps the glow of Father Grandier's burning was seen from the site. Richelieu himself looks down at us from many portraits: arrogant, proud, cunning and completely ruthless. He created the world of Louis XIV, and therefore the political climate which produced Versailles. It is to this new phase that we next turn.

VII

The Baroque Age, Late Baroque and Neo-Classicism

THE AGE OF BAROQUE

Introduction

Many cities and towns in Europe were adorned and transformed during the Baroque period. The impetus of baroque grew from Rome, and it spread throughout Europe and to the colonies of the great powers. In spite of its beginnings, it permeated Protestant as well as Roman Catholic societies. The last years of the renaissance and mannerist periods in Rome were years of terror, as Luther thundered from the north and Clement VII ascended the papal throne. It was as though a tepid and unwholesome south wind had caused a general distemper in the city, and some even asserted that Antichrist had come.[1] Paradoxically, however, after Charles V had intervened in papal affairs, monarchs rallied to the defence of the Pope, whose secular realm had been taken by a German–Spanish army, and secularization of the Papal States was postponed by the threat of the Reformation. The rise of Protestantism compelled the papacy to put its house in order and become once more the expression of spiritual power, and the nerve centre for a campaign against Protestantism. Allied with Roman Catholic princes, and regenerated itself, the papacy worked to recover what it had lost in terms of spiritual authority.

After 1527, new religious orders were founded: the Capuchins, Theatines, Piarists and the Jesuits; and new saints were added to the crown of the Church, including Charles Borromeo, Ignatius Loyola and Teresa of Avila. The renewal of spiritual energy was expressed in a gigantic building programme in Rome, which had lain semi-desolate for centuries.

Under Pope Sixtus V (1585–1590), baroque Rome began to appear in earnest. This pope was a symbol of the new spirit within the

---

[1] *The Civilization of the Renaissance in Italy* p. 66.

Church, for he came from a peasant family, unlike his immediate predecessors who had been members of the ruling classes. In less than five years he began a process of transformation of Rome which largely created the city we know today. His architects, Fontana and della Porta, began great avenues and vistas punctuated by obelisks and features, as well as completing the great cupola of Michelangelo's St. Peter's.

Under Sixtus, a unified planning scheme was devised for Rome to make it a splendid city once more, and to connect the main shrines for the convenience of pilgrims. The monumental achievement of Sixtus V was the Strada Felice which runs from the church of St. Trinita dei Monti to St. Maria Maggiore and on to St. Croce in Gerusalemme. The Spanish Steps were also planned during his pontificate, but were not built until the eighteenth century.

Many squares were built at this time, and most were adorned with obelisks, the most sensational of which was the re-erection of the antique Egyptian obelisk, which had once stood in a Roman circus, immediately before St. Peter's.

It is in individual buildings too that we see the beginning of the baroque movement. The great dome of St. Peter's was one of the first architectural expressions of the period, and Vignola's *Gesù* shows more than a beginning, but it was with the work of Bernini, Borromini and da Cortona that Roman baroque flowered.

The spirit of vehemence, of pathos, of passion and dark strength was seen in the remarkable Laocoön group which had been rediscovered in Michelangelo's day, and which made a profound impression on the artists of the time. Now, with the Church Militant and Rome regenerated, a new generation of architects came to work there. Circular motifs reappeared, and became even more subtle as ellipses in the hands of Bernini and Borromini. The latter's St. Carlo alle Quattro Fontane is a *tour de force* of architectural movement, for the whole building seems to sway, inside and out. Theatrical effects made their appearance too, especially in the *Scala Regia* of Bernini in the Vatican which adopts the techniques of the opera house to accentuate perspective. Astonishing too is Bernini's chapel in St. Maria della Vittoria which goes to extremes in illusionary method, for here St. Teresa in ecstasy is shown being pierced by a spear wielded by a smiling youthful angel, and her abandoned, voluptuous pose is illuminated by theatrical lighting and by gilded rods. This group is in turn watched by figures in theatrical boxes arranged round the chapel. The extreme theatricality of Bernini's work is also expressed in the gigantic Piazza of St. Peter's, where the huge colonnades stretch out from the early seventeenth century front of the church (by Maderna) to embrace the multitudes and the world. In the centre of the piazza is the obelisk erected by Sixtus V over sixty years before.

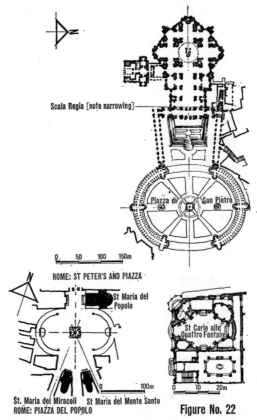

Scala Regia [note narrowing]

0   50   100   150m

ROME: ST PETER'S AND PIAZZA

St Maria del Popolo

St Carlo alle Quattro Fontane

Piazza di   San Pietro

100m

0   10   20m

St. Maria dei Miracoli   St Maria del Monte Santo
ROME: PIAZZA DEL POPOLO

Figure No. 22

The tensions and drama of baroque art express the political climate of the period, for the spirit of the Counter-Reformation was one of a militant re-conquest of the souls of men. Remembering that in the sixteenth century the symbols had been relegated to limbo and no longer expressed very much, we must also recall the rise of superstition with that of rationalism. As reality advanced so did unreason, so that a great dilemma was apparent in the seventeenth century. Freedom from symbolism had cheapened life itself, denying its sacramental significance and rendering symbols themselves of no account. The State had taken over, and God had retired, to be visited by proxy on Sundays. So it was that the metaphysical poets could write of the human spirit in terms such as:

'Thou art like a pilgrim, which abroad hath done
Treason, and durst not turne to whence hee is fled . . .,'[1]

ST TERESA IN ECSTASY
Sculptural group in the church of St Maria della
Vittoria, Rome (from a sketch by the author)

Figure No. 22a

and the separated parts of mankind's existence had to be directed towards each other once again to resolve the problem. To accomplish a reunion, violence had to be used, since violence had sundered the parts, and the daring theatrical bravado of the baroque

[1] *Holy Sonnets: Divine Meditations*, 2. (John Donne)

became the artistic expression of spiritual convolutions. The use of mandala forms became a potent weapon for the designers of the baroque period, and the central point closed heroic vistas. The piazza and dome of St. Peter's; the Piazza del Popolo; and all the circular and elliptical spaces of Roman buildings helped to focus on points of religious interest. Such vistas *from* a central point could extend to the horizon if desired, so opening up the country and embracing the world: now the dome bearing the words *Tu es Petrus* was not only the cover of the tomb of the Apostle, but the centre of yet another mandala form – the sphere of the world itself. The great dome was the centre from which radiated influences and sight lines in all possible directions . . . *Urbi et Orbi*.

Developments – Versailles and after
It was Louis XIII who first started using Versailles as a haven for himself and his mistress. The presence of the king and his retinue brought trade and prestige to the town. Richelieu's work near Chinon had set an example for future development, but the real model for Versailles was the vast estate of Minister Foucquet at Vaux, which had been laid out to the plans of Lemercier, Le Vau, Le Brun and Le Nôtre. After Louis XIV had become king, and Foucquet had created his residence, Louis had him arrested and himself acquired the architects, painter and gardener for his own schemes at Versailles.

The Louvre was uncomfortably near the evil-smelling Paris mob as well as being partly mediaeval, and it was impossible to create anything like Vaux or Richelieu in Paris. At Versailles, however, the king could build a new palace with landscaped gardens as a setting for the splendours of the French monarchy as well as to keep the nobility under his watchful eye. As the holder of absolute power, the king could reduce the nobility to mere ornaments at his court.

By 1682 the initial project had grown to the enormous palace with its formal grounds stretching to the horizon, while the town lay on the other side of the palace similarly laid out. The town, palace and gardens centred on the palace, as the point at which all radial axes meet. The palace became the central point in the composition and symbolized the total centralization of power in the person of the king.

The vistas of Rome had been one aspect, but now Versailles represented baroque planning on a vast scale, where the total en-

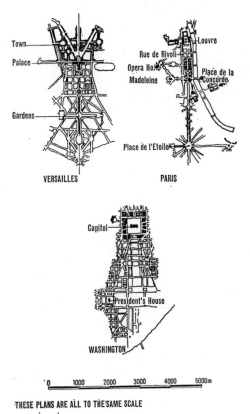

THESE PLANS ARE ALL TO THE SAME SCALE

Baroque legacy   Figure No. 23

vironment was unified forcibly, even brutally, by the use of radiating avenues and vistas in an enormous mandala conception, the centre of which was the personification of the state: King Louis XIV, *Le Roi Soleil*. The potential of baroque planning for propaganda as an expression of the power of the ruling classes must be stressed. The concepts of eye-stoppers and vistas to infinity both developed in the baroque period, and their combination in mandala forms could express centralization of political power. The opening up of the country with the town, so that all was dominated by a central point, is part of a characteristic attitude to spatial effects found at the time.

The importance of Versailles does not end with the place itself, but is magnified in that European monarchs thereafter attempted to emulate the French precedent. Things French became fashion-

Versailles (from a notebook by the author)   **Figure No. 23a**

able, and soon great palaces and vistas were appearing all over the
continent. France had earlier been the forerunner of town square
schemes, such as the Place des Vosges and the Place Dauphine, and
such examples of civic design had undoubtedly influenced other
plans such as the 'great piazza' at Covent Garden.

Wren's plan for London may definitely be seen as baroque, and
here the centre from which many roads and vistas radiated was to
be the Stock Exchange. As it happened, London's mediaeval plan
was preserved, and Wren gave us instead a magical skyline of
baroque, classical and Gothic spires, towers and pinnacles as well
as the enormous dominant of the dome of St. Paul's. More baroque
in plan was that of Greenwich, but the central axis is played down
so that where there should be a climax there is only the perfect little
Queen's House. The English always controlled the baroque, never
letting it reach the realms of complete extravagance that we find
in France, Italy, Germany or Spain. The creation of St. Paul's
expresses the power of the ruling elements, for St. Paul's was the
City Cathedral, and the churches had City connections with the
merchants and Guilds. 'Robbing Peter to pay Paul' referred to the
impoverishing of Westminster Abbey (the Collegiate Church of St.
Peter) to enrich St. Paul's. The churches express more civic pride
and political dominance of the great commercial interests than they
do the piety of the people, especially in an age when Mammon, the
King and the Nation-State had succeeded the Trinity in significance
in the lives of men. It must not be forgotten that in England Church
and State were combined, and the Church was controlled by political elements favoured by the ruling powers, so it expressed secular
rather than spiritual values.

CLEMENS VII· PONT· CCXXIII·
ANNO DOMINI MDXXIII·

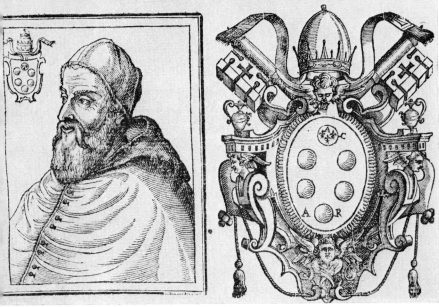

Plate 53: *Pope Clement VII.* (*Mansell Collection.*)

SIXTVS V· PONTIFEX CCXXXI·
ANNO DOMINI MDLXXXV·

Plate 54: *Pope Sixtus V.* (*Mansell Collection.*)

Plate 55: Laocoön. (Mansell Collection.)

Plate 56: St. Paul's Cathedral, London.

Plate 57: *Greenwich.*

Plate 58: *Salzburg from Schloss Mirabell.*

Plate 59: The Colonnade motif in Salzburg.

Plate 60: The Colonnade motif in Salzburg.

Plate 61 : The Immaculate Conception, Salzburg.

Plate 62 : Street leading to the Cathedral Square, Salzburg.

Plate 63: *The Cathedral Square, Salzburg.*

Plate 64: *Karlsruhe. The former Royal Palace.*

Plate 65: Karlsruhe.

Plate 66: Würzburg. Ecclesiastical power expressed in the approach to the town.

Plate 67 : The interior of the Bishop's Palace at Würzburg.

Plate 68 : The interior of the Bishop's Palace at Würzburg.

Plate 69: Melk.

Plate 70: Vienna. The Hofburg.

Plate 71 : The Library of the Hofburg, Vienna.

Plate 72 : The Hofburg, Vienna.

Plate 73: Salzburg, The Kollegienkirche.

Plate 74: Klosterneuburg.

Plate 75: Amorbach. The High Altar.

Plate 76: Amorbach. The organ.

Plate 77: Door detail forming a dignified entrance to a house in Spitalfields.

Plate 78: The Mall, Armagh. Irish Georgian.

Plate 79: Early 19th century housing in Clerkenwell.

Plate 80: Synagogue in Spitalfields.

Plate 81: Square in Clerkenwell. Designed by William Chadwell Mylne 1828.

Plate 82: Houses in Clerkenwell. Probably designed by John and William Joseph Booth 1819.

Plate 83: The Gardens at Kew. Pagoda designed by Sir William Chambers.

Plate 84: Percy Circus, near St. Pancras. Designed by William Chadwell Mylne c. 1842.

On the ecclesiastical side, we turn to Salzburg, since here was erected the first Italianate baroque building north of the Alps. The close and cathedral of SS. Rupert and Virgil were commenced in 1614 by Scamozzi and Solari. The scheme was held up by the Thirty Years War and was not completed until the middle of the century. Salzburg is a stunning example of a town dominated architecturally by the politically dominant group. High above the town is Hohensalzburg, a great rock crowned by the fortress of the Prince-Bishops, and the skyline at a lower level is punctuated by a myriad of towers, spires and domes. At ground level the inscape is one of great beauty. The colonnade motif appears everywhere in the city, not least in the cemeteries, and complexes of closed *Plätze* permeate the urban matrix. In the centre, round the splendid Cathedral, colonnades separate the cathedral square, with its central focus of the Immaculate Conception, from the Kapitelplatz, Marktplatz, Residenzplatz and Mozartplatz. The great archway that leads into

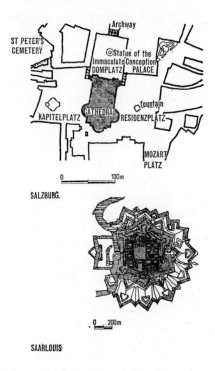

Baroque plans   Figure No. 24

the Domplatz beside the Bishop's Palace is a shattering motif, for the dark street, flanked by the tall buildings of a mediaeval Salzburg, suddenly bursts into a gleaming square with the white Cathedral towering above.

Germany and Central Europe were caught, as it were, in a 'pincer movement' of baroque ideas from France on the secular side and from Italy on the ecclesiastical. As well as the royal seat of Versailles, France provided another precedent for European planners with the fortified towns on the eastern frontier associated with the name of Vauban. Saarlouis, perhaps the best known example of Vauban's work, had an area of fortification much greater than that of the actual town. Under Louis XIV, many towns were replanned and enriched by the Intendants or provincial governors, who were charged with the erection of public buildings, laying out of roads and the beautifying of towns within their jurisdiction. This, no doubt, was for the greater glory of France, and therefore of the king.

In Germany, Karl Wilhelm of Baden founded in 1715 a new town with obvious debts to both Versailles and to Vitruvian ideas. At the very centre of a circular plan is the tower of the monarch's palace, and town and gardens are divided up by radii of the circle which create segments of town and country. The town, Karlsruhe (Karl's Rest), thus centres on the palace, the dominant of which is the central tower. Egocentric though the plan may look, in fact Karlsruhe is a gentle, unassuming place, reflecting the attitudes of its founder and descendents who were inclined to liberal–intellectual views. The architecture of the palace is definitely not an overbearing expression of absolutism, although the town plan would lead us to believe the opposite. Thus it must be stressed that inscape, character, detail must be studied with the plan itself in making an assessment of the contemporary Zeitgeist. Mannheim owes something to Versailles too, for the rebuilt city (1699 and after) was arranged on a main axis which ran through the centre of the palace. The town plan, however, is a gridiron and is more related to Scamozzi's *città ideale* with a royal palace superimposed.

Ansbach had its palace added in rococo times, and is for many the most perfect of all secular rococo buildings (1726–1740).

An interesting feature of the baroque age was the development of formal pleasure gardens associated with the palaces and great houses. A common item in such gardens was the maze, which was a variant of the ancient labyrinth which was known in Minoan and

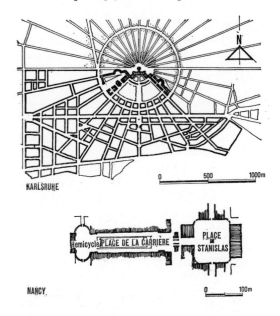

KARLSRUHE

NANCY

Karlsruhe and Nancy   : Figure No. 25

Celtic civilizations, and appeared again in the designs of floors in mediaeval cathedrals. The labyrinth design is a mandala form, and may have been a symbol of the Holy Grail since it represented pilgrimages which were symbolic themselves of the Christian journey through life to fulfilment. On a small scale in baroque and rococo gardens it was an instrument of the illusion of depth and infinity, and so it had certain affinities with the mirror, another favourite baroque motif.

Inter-related *places* are found at Nancy, residence of Stanislas, exiled King of Poland, and these spaces are related formally on axes. The designer, Héré de Corny, built the Nancy complex between 1752 and 1755, unifying the various elements in a wonderful sequence of spaces. The total concept is called the *Place Royale* and includes a hemicycle dedicated to Louis XV. The idea of a *Place Royale* occurred often in eighteenth-century French planning. Such *places* were designed geometrically, were enclosed by buildings and 'glorified the greatness of the monarchy,' often being enriched with monuments to the kings.[1] Other great *places* included the Place des

---

[1] *The West European City* p. 435.

Victoires (1685–1687), and the Place Vendôme which was built by
Mansard after he had completed Versailles. In Paris, however, the
most far-reaching of all the schemes was the formation of a great
axis to the Louvre which was connected across county with the axis
of Versailles. It was named the Champs Élysées.

The power of the monarchy as the dominant in society is amply
demonstrated by the plans and monuments of French towns and
cities. In Germany, too, the ruling classes were celebrated in the
palaces and vistas of the eighteenth century. Dresden, with its
Zwinger of 1711–1722, is a supreme example of building on a vast
scale as a backcloth for the pageants of the court of Augustus,
Elector of Saxony, King of Poland, most noted glutton, soldier and
fornicator extraordinary. The Zwinger is a huge symmetrical
orangery consisting of galleries linking pavilions of the most luscious
and voluptuous extravagance, encrusted in baroque ornamentation
in a riot of imaginative fantasy.

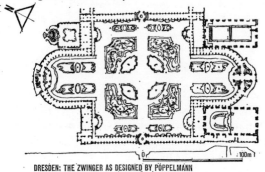

DRESDEN: THE ZWINGER AS DESIGNED BY POPPELMANN

Dresden and Edinburgh   Figure No. 26

The Zwinger Palace at Dresden (after a sketch by the author)   Figure No. 26a

At Würzburg, ecclesiastical and secular power are combined in the great Prince-Bishop's palace of the Schönborns, which owes a debt to Versailles, but is transformed into something far more human. The interior is full of marvellous things, not least the great ceiling by Tiepolo.

The Church militant and triumphant can be found expressed at Melk in the Danube valley. This gigantic monastery, perched on a cliff high above the river, was begun in 1702 by Prandtauer, and dominates the little town below. Melk is *Kloster und Burg* transformed from grim citadel to a *tour de force* of strength, joy and ecstatic fulfilment. A town in itself, it possesses a vast church, with a dome and twin towers, flanked by two wings which shoot forward to the edge of the precipice. They are joined by a mighty triumphal arch. Astonishingly, inside, the library, church, rooms and courts are palatial: one could be in the Schönborn's palace at Würzburg or even in Maria Theresia's Hofburg, but it is a monastery. Secular art and sacred art converged, so that in the Holy Roman Empire the same standards of magnificence were applied to both palace and monkish retreat. At Klosterneuburg, Ettal and St. Florian, similar magnificent monasteries were built, symbolic of the renewed power of the Church.

The Karlskirche, Vienna
(from a drawing by the author)   **Figure No. 26b**

In Vienna, after the Turkish menace had been removed, the Hapsburgs attempted to emulate the Bourbons, as is seen in early schemes for Schönbrunn by Johann Bernhardt Fischer von Erlach, while Prince Eugen was presented with Hildebrandt's Belvedere. Vienna and the surrounding territories were enriched at the beginning of the eighteenth century by an astonishing outburst of building activity. The Hofburg in Vienna was extended and acquired the magnificent library, and von Erlach built the extraordinary Karlskirche (1716–1729). This church is an expression of two things: militant and triumphant Roman Catholicism, and the imperial pride of the Empire's capital. The twin Trajanesque columns celebrating the activities of the baroque saint Charles Borromeo, an elliptical dome, a portico and two extravagant pavilions all combine to form one of the strangest and most memorable compositions of the Baroque Age. Fischer von Erlach also enriched Salzburg: the wilful Kollegienkirche and the Dreifaltigkeitskirche are his work also.

One of the most baroque things in baroque Vienna is the tomb of the Kaiserin Maria Theresia and her consort, Franz I, in the

Hapsburg vaults. This work, by Balthasar Moll, finished in 1754, is stunning, for the royal couple are depicted as living, in the marriage bed, draped in splendid garments, while a cherub, armed with the *Tuba mirum*, presents them with flowers.

We have seen how the baroque period opened up new vistas, embracing infinity and the horizon in terms of planning. Similarly, illusion and theatrical tricks were used to accentuate a point in a design. The twin churches of the Piazza del Popolo in Rome draw attention to the central obelisk, and the triumphal arch at Melk leads the eye inevitably to the church.

Illusions were used inside buildings too, for the baroque artists were concerned primarily with space, or its denial, as well as with a renewal of the significance of symbols. What do the Lily among Thorns, Star above Woods, and, most poignant of all, the Mystic Rose, mean to us today? In baroque art, ideas of Faith, of Hope and of Charity take on human shape; secular arms and flags protect the Cross, while the Keys, Tiara and Mitre combine with Seasons, Elements and Virtues in a panorama of endless virtuosity and never-ceasing movement. In late baroque times, Marian symbols of the Fountain and the Rose occur again and again in ceilings and stucco work in both profane and sacred buildings, so that after we become aware of the recurring themes and have achieved the heightened perception and sensibility that prolonged acquaintance with such images bring, we are able to enter a baroque world with understanding and historical imagination. Almost disembodied, we become drugged with the autumnal enchantment of baroque culture, its violence and its later rococo gentleness. The inexpressible longing to understand each nuance is strong in us, and we become conscious that a fusion of symbol and reality was achieved by violence. The denial of spatial logic is in itself a breaking down of conventional form, and reality and illusion merge into a total experience.

There comes a time when we can no longer tell if we are in a palace or a church, for the same symbols proliferate as they pass the barriers of reality. When the wonder of it is understood, its significance wells up in an unspeakable rightness, for the unimagined and the unimaginable can be seen, felt and experienced. Being part of life, of the cosmos, of creation, we are linked undeniably with the totality, and space no longer exists as something terrifying, and life has a changed meaning. Unity is again achieved, as we are reconciled to the inevitability and order of things, and with an erotic sense of completeness we can savour the intensity of the baroque vision of the world and beyond. Looking up at the ceiling at Würzburg, Wies, Vierzehnheiligen or any of the finer churches or palaces, it is with a sense of surprise that we see how high the clouds really are, yet we could touch them if we had a ladder. The blueness in the white formations is yet as deep as it is possible to experience. As the rococo dawned, so the mood, like the Zeitgeist, became lighter, with gaiety mingled with a controlled pathos where once there had been dark and violent passions. The profane and the sacred unite, for the difference in baroque and rococo art is only one of emphasis. A chapel becomes a porcelain room; a high altar becomes a shepherdess's bower; and an asymmetrical mirror, carried by a cluster of rococo babies reflects ourselves, and the many facets of life and art combine like the colours in the spectrum to form a completeness that is as clear as the light itself flooding in through windows. This mirror is a variant of the mandala idea.[1]

LATER DEVELOPMENTS

In England in the mid-eighteenth century, much town development took place as speculative enterprise for the housing of a new class made rich by trade. Georgian Bath grew as a place for the residence and entertainment of this new class, and it was largely the work of the Woods, father and son. The unified circuses, crescents, squares and terraces are composed of standardized units, and they owed no dependence to a dominant element of either ecclesiastical or secular origin. These housing groups were strong elements themselves, and expressed the wealth of the new middle classes, but at the same time the schemes were of a high quality, probably because of the traditions of craftsmanship and the fact that a mode of detail and manners in design were universally accepted.

A similarity between Georgian developments and those at Versailles a century earlier was the juxtaposition of natural and artificial; Rousseau had praised nature and the 'natural man', and the renewed relationship between the house and nature may have been partly due to widespread interest in Rousseau's ideas, although in England there had been traditions of closeness to nature due to the less urbanized society which existed.

---

[1] In baroque times, the same music was often used for both secular and religious occasions, for example, the works of J. S. Bach.

Just as in Hellenic times there had been a turning to Dionysus, so a new Age of Reason in the seventeenth and eighteenth centuries brought about an equal and opposite reaction: interest was revived in the occult and therefore in the country, nature, forests and wilds since the latter represented the antithesis of the reasoned town. The relationship with greenery was impossible in the old walled towns, but as fortification became more obsolete, or the political unit became safe internally, so great gardens could develop, and, in the case of Georgian England, so could the squares and gardens.

The squares of London and Edinburgh, Dublin and Glasgow represent the changing of cities by the architecture of a new middle class. The confidence and sureness of touch in such developments express the political significance of this social group. There is a quiet dignity in the squares of the Georgian period, where the simple dwelling units are connected with a piece of country in the form of a closed square in the centre. These squares were used communally by the tenants of the houses in the square, for, after the first quarter of the eighteenth century, inhabitants of squares had the powers to enclose them and keep them in order. It is interesting to note that in Bloomsbury, squares are inter-related in a non-axial fashion, unlike French examples.

Perhaps one of the greatest schemes of the eighteenth century in the British Isles was Craig's Edinburgh New Town of 1767. George Street, with Charlotte Square and St. Andrew Square at each end, each with a central monument, had its axis terminated to the east by the Bank, and to the west by St. George's Church, a typical baroque device. Eighteenth-century Glasgow must have been exceptionally fine. The slums of the Gorbals were actually overcrowded eighteenth-century upper–middle class houses, but even today the remains of some splendid eighteenth-century developments may be seen, and in the graveyard behind St. Mungo's Cathedral a Grecian necropolis on the hill stuns us into a state of disbelief, for here the wealthy middle classes left us a monument to their wealth and power which has outlived the houses they inhabited when alive.

The remarkable fact is that in neither individual buildings nor in plan in Bloomsbury residential developments is there a hint of the monumental. Bloomsbury was developed over 150 years, and formed despite this a simply woven fabric of urban design, to a very human scale. It has, of course, been ruined by London University, whose vast dominant tower glowers over the whole district. Bloomsbury, like other great eighteenth-century developments, was laid out for aristocratic owners by various architects, builders and speculators as the residential districts of a growing and prosperous middle class. Rents were on long leases and the open spaces were communal, so a unity of character was obtained.

Even with the nineteenth century, such a tradition of architectural unity was continued, and nature was integrated in the scheme, as residential development continued north and east of Bloomsbury towards St. Pancras and Islington. Some charming nineteenth-century houses still exist in Clerkenwell, dating from the 1830's and '40's and these all preserve the Georgian tradition.

Unity of architectural units was maintained by Nash in his great schemes for Regent's Park, where nature is again part of the design, and he joined this via Portland Place[1] to Regent Street and thence to St. James' Park and the great terraces of Carlton House. At the end of the Mall was the façade of a much more splendid palace than stands today. According to Giedion, these residential developments in Regent's Park and other places in Regency times were for an 'opulent and anonymous class who had been made rich by industry . . . trade . . . or the exploitation of English victories in the field.'[2]

Significantly, these new terraces were designed to look like great palaces, and were enriched with classical ornament, whereas Bloomsbury had been simple and unadorned. The pride of victory is here, and the opulence of a growing imperial power, sure of itself, is reflected in the houses of its influential citizens. Nash planned similar developments at Prinny's watering place of Brighton. The great terraces and squares of a town made fashionable by the First Gentleman reflect the desire of the new and richer middle class to emulate the aristocracy. This monumentalized development was to be carried on in Kensington and Paddington in the Victorian age.

We have mentioned French examples, and we have mentioned Vauban. The latter is interesting for matters other than fortifications, for he was aware of the dangers of ignoring the needs of the mass of the people, and indeed fell from his monarch's favour by drawing his attention to the need not to ignore the majority of the people. Vauban and others were not heeded, however, and French planning was primarily interested, as we have seen, in the building of *places* and great avenues. While such items had priority, the old

---

[1]   1778 by the Brothers Adam.
[2]   *Space, Time and Architecture* p. 637.

capital, Paris, sank into overcrowding and squalor, with the exceptions of the few avenues and squares mentioned previously.

When the Revolution began in 1789, the old régime was removed together with its symbols, including the Bastille, many royalist monuments, toll houses and gates. The problems of the future, caused by the opening of the towns, were not foreseen, yet the removal of such sharp breaks between town and country as toll houses and gates marked the beginnings of a subsequent growth of urban sprawl.

At first it seemed that the new political climate of the Revolution would encourage secular, civic and democratic schemes in place of those of a royal character. Instead, the despotism of the monarchy was replaced by the tyranny of the Terror. The revolutionary government confiscated the city land holdings of the king, nobility and clergy, executing thousands in the process, since confiscation was thought not to be enough. A Commission of Artists was formed charged with replanning Paris with better communications, more markets and the improvement of slums. This Commission proposed the opening up of long streets, an idea at once appreciated by Napoleon. One of the problems of governing in Paris was that of keeping the mob at bay. The Bastille, symbol of monarchist oppression, had fallen in 1789, and gentle, ineffectual Louis XVI's head, symbol of monarchy, the anointed brow, symbol of the divine right of kings, followed in 1793, victim of Madame Guillotine. Louis, imbued with liberal ideas from Rousseau and Voltaire, had shown sympathy for the people and adopted a pacific line. Napoleon, as a commoner, had less respect for the masses, referring to them as *canaille*,[1] and kept them in order by means of military power. Aristotle knew that irregular streets were very good for keeping soldiery at bay: so did Napoleon, who enthusiastically commenced implementing the plans of the Commission of Artists. He started with the Rue de Rivoli, and commissioned Percier and Fontaine to design it. This avenue begins in the Place de la Concorde, and the architecture was unified in a continuous composition. The Rue de Rivoli was strategically important for troop movements, and work on it was followed by the smaller streets of Castiglioni, de la Paix and others, as well as three new parts of the Quais along the river. Under Napoleon, the city was further ornamented, the most important items being the forecourt to St. Sulpice, the Temple of Glory (later

[1] *Civic Art* p. 244.

the Madeleine), the Arc de Triomphe on the Place de l'Étoile, and the huge column in the Place Vendôme.[1] Significantly, the Napoleonic Zeitgeist was expressed in its late baroque planning, its Empire style and its neo-classicism in art and architecture. Napoleon abolished the Holy Roman Empire, but he himself was crowned Emperor of the French, the Pope being present at the coronation to preserve continuity, but Bonaparte was careful to place the crown on his own head to symbolize that he owed allegiance to no one. Sculpture, painting and architecture became more and more reminiscent of Imperial Rome, and statues and medallions of Napoleon appeared which were based entirely on Roman prototypes. Triumphal arches, columns, and heroic groups of statuary completed the resemblance.

The Carrousel Arch is at one end of the Champs Élysées, and the enormous Arc de Triomphe is at the other, beyond which is the Boulevard de la Grande Armée. The scale of these Parisian vistas is superhuman, symbolic of the larger than life imperial ambition. I experimented with walking along these boulevards, starting with the Arc de Triomphe in sight: there it is, ahead, then after ages and ages and a very long walk, it is hardly any nearer, so the process is exhausting. The Paris of Napoleon and his successors is a Paris for processions, armies, parades, carriages: it is not for pedestrians.

Hegemann points out that the political decision to replan Paris shifted the centre of the city from the Palais Royal to the boulevards between the Faubourg du Temple and the Madeleine.[1] What Napoleon and the Commission of Artists started, Napoleon III and Baron Haussmann completed. The new Emperor, who had achieved power on a wave of popular emotion, was to consolidate that power by means, among others, of town planning improvements. In the 1848 Revolution, a garrison had been isolated, and artillery could not be used against the mob in the old streets. Long, wide thoroughfares, ideal for accurate shooting by the military, would no doubt inhibit the revolutionary fervour of future Parisians. This new Napoleon, like his uncle a son of revolution, well knew the value of protection from within as well as the fact that magnificent display and a furious show of constructional activity always convince the people of the excellence of a government much more than liberal attitudinizing. Pomp and display and a lot of noise rouse the *hoi-polloi* to heights of patriotic or partisan enthu-

---

[1] *Civic Art* p. 244.

siasm, and such theatricals are always in evidence in totalitarian states, even if an emperor is replaced by a party chairman, dictator or president. The will of Napoleon III was largely accomplished by Baron Georges-Eugène Haussmann, described by Persigny as having a 'backbone of iron', who had the audacity and ruthlessness necessary for his task. At first a commission of experts on town planning matters was set up, but Haussmann found the speeches and procedures of committees tedious, so had the commission abolished. The result was an expenditure of fantastic energy which created modern Paris, an example of what a dictator can achieve, for visible, impressive results were obtained, and paid no regard to what was there already except the monumental avenues which were too large to ignore. In a sense, Haussmann's boulevards represent order forced on a jungle – the wild jungle of old Paris, but despite all its faults, the Paris of Napoleon III remains an exercise in civic grandeur, and rather a splendid one, even if the architecture is only stucco, and the house and apartments were cramped. The quality of the tree-shaded streets of Paris is still worth a great deal in an age when we are desperately afraid of formalism.

In 1791 Peter Charles L'Enfant produced a plan for Washington, the new capital of the young United States of America. Essentially, this plan is a design of two axes intersecting at right angles, each with its own foci, the White House and the Capitol. Diagonal boulevards accentuate the foci, and a background of gridiron pattern is superimposed over the whole. The diagonals cut through this pattern, providing star-shaped points from which boulevards radiate, a very baroque form. The rectangular plots and gridiron plan may have been suggested by Thomas Jefferson, who designed much eighteenth-century American architecture, and the resulting plan of Washington may well express the combination of late baroque planning on the French model (which to contemporaries would have suggested liberty, equality and fraternity rather than absolutism), with the urbane colonial Georgian manner of the civilized Mr. Jefferson. Although the combination of diagonals and gridiron is most unfortunate, for it causes a number of impossible sites at awkward junctions, the plan of Washington symbolizes the aspirations of the new republic admirably. On the main axis is the Capitol, and on the secondary axis is the White House, the two buildings of the two great political powers of the state. L'Enfant made the president's house the centre of seven radiating boulevards, but as Hegemann points out, this was probably as much as to 'serve the pleasure of the president himself' as for the enjoyment of the public.[1] An egocentric plan to us smacks of absolutism, but in the political climate of the late eighteenth century such a device stemming from Revolutionary France would have savoured of democracy.

French neo-classicism influenced such German architects as Klenze, Semper, Schinkel and Gilly. After Piranesi, a monumental style developed in the late eighteenth century in designs by Boullée and Ledoux. These two designers had expressed an interest in the ordinary mass of the people and had reduced ornament to a minimum. Boullée's designs show a megalomaniac vastness where scale had ceased to be human at all. His designs for cemeteries, cenotaphs and a cathedral express the search for an architecture of the emotions, with grandeur and magic, hence his introduction of motifs such as spheres, obelisks and pyramids. The design of buildings serving some collective purpose, such as civic centres and cemeteries, was expressed in as grandiose a fashion as possible, for to Boullée the individual was of little account: what mattered was the mass, of people or building. Ledoux designed an ideal city with public buildings such as a palace of moral values, and this plan was an ellipse with roads separated from houses, so that this design may be regarded as a forerunner of the 'garden city', since green wedges and belts are incorporated in the design. Ledoux is also interesting for his use of the forms of Greece and Rome with a freedom which was matched in England by Soane and by Gilly in Prussia.

Soane's Bank of England is an astonishing work, austere and strong, rather like a citadel, while his house in Lincoln's Inn Fields is a lesson in the complexities of spatial organization. Gilly produced a number of interesting designs, among which must be included the national monument to Frederick the Great; a national theatre for Berlin and a scheme for a coastal town in which strong axes link sea, horizon, city and mountains. Gilly and Soane were originals and were truly 'modern' designers who used forms boldly and adapted classical motifs to their own needs. Unlike the French, they produced designs that were human in scale, and not megalomaniac exercises in the glorification of the collective ideas of 'state', 'people' and 'revolution'.

Prussia adopted the French style when eighteenth-century Berlin was laid out with the great ceremonial way of the Unter den Linden,

[1] *Civic Art* p. 291.

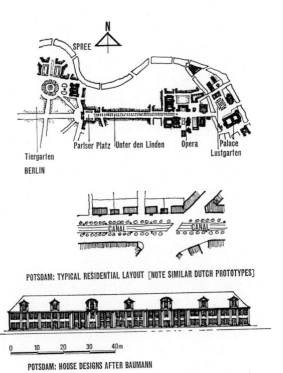

POTSDAM: TYPICAL RESIDENTIAL LAYOUT [NOTE SIMILAR DUTCH PROTOTYPES]

POTSDAM: HOUSE DESIGNS AFTER BAUMANN

Berlin and Potsdam　　　　　　　**Figure No. 27**

the palace by Schlüter, the Opera Square and the Brandenburg Gate. Potsdam was also largely an eighteenth-century town created by Frederick William I, his son Frederick the Great, and the architects Baumann and G. W. von Knobelsdorff. The incomparably delicious Sans Souci, the *Chinoiserie* in the gardens, the gentle, civilized terraces of houses speak to us more eloquently of the taste and humanity of the creators of Potsdam than we would be led to believe by prejudices against 'Prussianism'. The town was not only a place for the living quarters of the crack troops for Frederick's army, but it was also the seat of the king of Prussia, who was an enlightened despot.

The baroque had a universal vision, and it did not shrink from attempting to re-fuse the Noösphere and the Biosphere by violent means. A mystical vision could be realized just as Bernini had done at Rome with the ecstasy of St. Teresa. The facility for moulding space and dominating it, or allowing it to dominate, was understood by the self-confident designers of the time. Nature was pulled into the scheme of things, regulated where necessary and allowed to be unregulated at other times. In England, 'unregulated landscapes' were designed by Shenstone, Repton, Brown and others as part of a new movement away from French and Italian classicism, but in true baroque art between man-made constructed objects and organic things there was a bond symbolized in the mandala forms of cities, buildings and the world. Such mandala forms had reaffirmed the totality of experience in the symbol, and in baroque and rococo art symbols abounded. Their realism is the property of an art that describes, elevates and explains, and in so doing reveals to us the truth of what *is* reality. The 'English landscape' was a Romantic movement, and therefore was a trend away from the great European art-synthesis.

Those enchanted autumnal days of an age which produced Mozart, Fragonard, the Zwinger, Vierzehnheiligen and Sans Souci represent the last part of an epoch which was destroyed by its own turning to rationalism. After the high point of a creative period symbolized by a Laocoön, a St. Teresa, a *Nozze di Figaro*, a Vierzehnheiligen, comes a period in which a culture looks back to become neo-classical, then Romantic, and finally, confused with its own eclecticism, tired, bored to death, it succumbs to new alien influences, and rushes to its own destruction by opening its arms to an invader or by being too weak to resist.

It was Goethe who saw the dangers lying in wait for the civilization of the eighteenth century. Horrified by Schiller's 'Robbers' and by a Zeitgeist created by his own contemporaries, he warned us of the damage done by reason, for ideas would make a model of an ideal which in no time at all would be set up as a truth. Eighteenth century reason had brought forth monsters, and Romanticism was born. A revived Church was challenged by philosophers, so that 'enlightenment' and 'rationalism' developed which were splendid for the intelligentsia, but disastrous for the people. The reasoning of the eighteenth century destroyed the mysteries once again, which became warped and unholy. So the chaos of romanticism developed, and thousands of styles were revived; Gothick horrors were boiled up from the hungry longings of a society in need of mystery. Goethe warned that confused ideas give birth to confused deeds, and the final result would be the disruption of the totality of experience where aesthetic, moral and religious values which once had been whole would now be compartmented. No longer held in symbols, the symbols themselves declined in significance and became allegorical and lost all reason for existing. So the cities and towns themselves became mixtures of all that archaeology could provide, and they began to lose their forms as well as their innate qualities, which had given them their inscapes and made them works of art.

VIII

The Beginnings of Modern Development

INTRODUCTION

A new phase of urbanization began in Britain in the eighteenth century with the Industrial and Agrarian Revolutions, but Europe was not affected much until the middle of the nineteenth century, and it was then too that the great urban units of America began to expand and develop.

From the middle of the eighteenth century the population of the British Isles began to rise rapidly, due to a fall in the death-rate. A decline in infant mortality altered the proportions of size of generations and thus changed fundamentally the structure of society. The fall in the death-rate was due to several factors, among which may be mentioned better nutrition; better personal hygiene made possible by the increased uses of soap and cheap cotton garments; better building construction; the decline of cottage industries; better drains and water supply; and concern for refuse disposal and the burial of the dead.

The traditional methods of agricultural production were wasteful and inefficient, and existing patterns of settlement could no longer support growing populations, so younger members of the community were forced to seek work elsewhere. The discovery that turnips could be used to feed cattle in the winter obviated the necessity for wholesale slaughter of beasts as had been the practice until that time, and fresh meat became available throughout the winter months. New methods of selective cattle breeding; the improvement of ploughing and sowing techniques; and the introduction of clover as a soil-regenerator profoundly affected the economy of rural Britain and its settlement pattern. The support of a growing population was made possible by such innovations, but the method of carrying out the reforms caused terrible hardship. The Enclosure Acts deprived the yeomanry of their rights, making them either tenant farmers or labourers, or driving them off the land altogether to seek work in industry.

The traditional cottage industries were too diffused to provide the goods to meet the tremendous growth in demand. The invention of machinery for spinning and weaving driven first by hand, then by water, and finally by steam, sealed the fate of the cottage industries and concentrated industry in factories. These factories, sited near water and coal deposits, encouraged migration from the agricultural settlements so that new urban developments mushroomed. In most cases these growths were just thrown together, and industrial waste and poor layout began to create that desolation so characteristic of nineteenth century industrial towns.

After the Enclosure Acts and the deprivation of the yeomen of their ancient rights, the class differences were accentuated, wealth being concentrated in fewer hands, and the free men and their families became the proletariat, forming the labour factor of production. The politically dominant families, however, already rich, became richer, and the creation of 'romantick Landskips' was helped by the emptying of the country. Numbers of displaced farmers went abroad to the New World, where largely virgin territory awaited them. In Ireland, the conacre system[1] had pauperized a population almost as large as that of England and Wales, and the desperate search for land may be understood by studying the deserted farmlands at high altitudes, especially in Co. Fermanagh, which had a population of over 156,000 in 1841 declining by 1961 to just over 50,000 people.

Rural depopulation was caused by several factors, but one which is often overlooked, probably because of a romantic notion of the charms of country life, was the fact that the urban slums were probably a lot better than the rural ones. The character of rural housing was poorest in Ireland, in the Highlands of Scotland and in Wales, and the unbelievable squalor of the Irish homestead was a real and terrible fact. Often the houses were built of turf with only a hole to let the smoke out, while a pit in the ground outside the entrance served as privy and midden. Neither rain nor cold was kept out, and such cabins were common until the Great Famine solved the overcrowding problem in Ireland. The misery of Irish country life was prolonged by the conacre system, absentee landlords, and agents who soaked the peasantry of all they possessed. At the other end of the social scale were the great landowners of the Anglo-Irish upper classes, including prelates of the Church of Ireland such as

[1] Short-term rent of 11 months. See *Land Use in Northern Ireland* pp. 19, 38, 43, 157, 176–181.

the Lord Bishop of Derry,[1] whose two huge country houses were models of the most magnificent of eighteenth century mansions. Downhill was said to be larger than Blenheim, and Ballyscullion has only left us the portico which now adorns the front of the Church of St. George in Belfast. Florencecourt is another example of the great Irish country seat, while Armagh provides us with a charming eighteenth century town enriched by Dr. Robinson, Archbishop from 1767. Architects such as Cooley and Johnston were engaged, and Armagh, by the early years of the nineteenth century, was one of the finest towns in Ireland. It is interesting that in Ireland, where the majority of the population in the southern and western parts of the country was Roman Catholic, dominant buildings, including religious ones, were associated with the ruling Protestant classes. In Belfast, enlightened non-conformist liberals contributed to the first Roman Catholic church to be built in the town, but it was not until after Catholic emancipation that the Roman Catholics were able to erect numbers of churches, most of them dating from the mid-nineteenth century. The timing was unfortunate, for the churches could hardly have been built at a worse time architecturally, and with few exceptions, Roman Catholic churches in Ireland are not notable for their qualities. A significant expression of the dominant and differing powers in Ireland is found in Armagh, the ecclesiastical capital. On a hill in the centre of the town is the Cathedral of the Church of Ireland, symbolic of *Kloster* and *Burg*. On another hill just outside the bounds of the original town is the Roman Catholic Cathedral, a revival of French Gothic. The two cathedrals vie with each other across the valley, and are symbolic of the split in religious life in Ireland.

Several landowners endeavoured to improve the housing conditions of their tenants, and when, in 1812, Caledon House was reconstructed by Nash, the village was rebuilt as a model town. Sadly, it is now in a state of decay, many of the houses being roofless as depopulation continues apace, accentuated by the nearness of the political frontier, which has amputated much of the hinterland.

After the 'Hungry Forties' when Ireland lost hundreds of thousands of people as a result of the potato blight and subsequent starvation and emigration, the factory system came to Ireland too, and the drift from the land became a stampede, especially after the

---

[1] His absentee habits will be brought home when we consider the number of hotels called after him throughout Europe. Although Lord Bishop of Derry, he was also the Earl of Bristol, hence the name 'Hotel Bristol'.

repeal of the Corn Laws and the breaking up of the great estates.[1]

Of great importance in the nineteenth century reform movement was John Grubb Richardson, who established Bessbrook, near Newry, in 1846. A Quaker, Richardson planned a pub-less, police-less town with houses built round open greens, a community centre and a mill. Richardson's work was an example to Cadbury, and pre-dates Saltaire, Victoria and all the famous mid-Victorian model villages and towns. The Quakers were also active with experimental settlements in Glentone, Co. Galway, in an endeavour to alleviate the problems of abject poverty and starvation of the rural community as well as to eradicate the 'demon drink', a well-known Irish curse.[2]

The sorrows of Ireland were greater than those of England, for it was not until the 1840's that the industries managed to take some of the surplus population off the land in any numbers, whereas industrialization had begun in earnest in eighteenth century England. In a generation, technical advances had developed so quickly that a host of towns grew near the factories of the north and midlands. Although the proletariat was undoubtedly exploited by industrialists, having first been robbed by the landowners who controlled Parliament, a wide choice of possible employment was available in the industrial centres, and by the third decade of the nineteenth century, workers were organizing themselves into bodies for mutual protection.

Crucial to the development of the new industries and towns was the need for communications to be improved. The turnpikes had begun a process which was to continue with the building of the canal system and the railways. A modern transport system encouraged the explosion of urbanism, trade and industry, and quickened the whole tempo of life. Soon the dominants were the chimneys and huge factories, pithead gears, slag heaps and great engineering works of canal and railway. Canal buildings had a strength of their own, and exploit techniques of mass-production and standard detailing in the ironwork of the aqueducts, while railways cut gashes through the countryside and blighted hundreds of acres of land. Modern ideas in structure were exploited in the great railway bridges and termini, however, and contributed to future architectural development. The new dominants represented the reality and

---

[1] For further information, see *Rural Life in Northern Ireland* and *Town and Country in Northern Ireland*.
[2] The *North British Mail*, June 20th, 1849.

new scale of industrial development, while huddled near the factories and under the shadow of the chimneys were the houses of the workers. The relationship has similarities to that of the castle and houses in mediaeval times, except that in the nineteenth century, the dominant was the place of work and only source of livelihood for the majority of the people living near it. The new owners of capital and their middle-men exhibited their wealth in the villas and mansions on the outskirts of the towns, built in every imaginable style and non-style. Eclecticism was going berserk.

Human life became paradoxically more valuable at this time, for there is evidence by Ireland and others that the children of the very poor had been permitted to die while babies, if not actually murdered at birth. The new system, however, encouraged the employment of children, so that decline in infant mortality may have been directly related to the commercial value of the child on the labour market.[1]

The Napoleonic Wars which ended in 1815 had been responsible for inflation and a tremendous rise in costs. The end of the Wars threatened the monopolies of merchants and farmers in Britain, with the result that the country became protectionist and isolationist. Military success was mirrored in the monumental classicism of Regency housing developments, but the inhabitants of these developments feared a re-arising of revolutionary forces which, it was hoped, had been defeated in the field. It must be remembered that at the time influences from the French Revolution were looked on with almost hysterical horror, since the ruling classes of Britain tended to be aristocratic, wealthy and landowning, or middle class, wealthy and capital owning, while the Revolution savoured of the mob. The establishment tended to be also associated with Anglicanism in England, while radical ideas often stemmed from nonconformists. In eighteenth century England, the Opposition to the Government consisted of another group of similar people. The French Revolution had, in fact, been a practical application of the views of English non-conformist intellectuals, and this may explain the single-mindedness with which the wars were pursued, England being allied with all the monarchies of Europe in order to crush the Revolution. Nothing else would explain the restoration of the discredited Bourbons and the mutual bolstering up of the ancient kingdoms and Empires, for 'balance of power' theories do

[1] *A Prospect of Cities* p. 141.

not bear close inspection. After the Wars, and especially after 1832, the ruling classes found it prudent to draw the middle classes into co-operation with them, so that the new society dominated by business interests would not upset the real holders of power. The dangling of such carrots as royal decorations and ennoblements in front of the bourgeoisie ensured the pacification of the rising middle classes who were thus brought within the framework of tradition.[1] Fear of displacement made the governing classes act repressively with unusual vigour. The 1798 rebellion in Ireland, largely led by Protestant intellectuals[2] of middle class origins, was put down with savagery by the authorities, all the ringleaders being executed. An Act of Union was passed two years later which abolished the separate Irish parliament and caused Dublin to decline, as it was no longer a capital.

The wealth, prosperity and respectability of the property-owning influential classes contrasted somewhat with the squalid quarters of the working classes, so further mutual suspicion grew. The building of houses and the conversion of existing premises as dwellings for the workers were carried out to minimum standards. Rents were low, and linked to low wages, since the profit-motive was the *raison d'être* of the factories, so quality in design and construction could not be very good, yet, as we have seen, the housing in the towns was probably better than that in the rural areas. The problems grew, however, in other directions, for poor or non-existent sanitation, while possible in country districts, was concentrated and multiplied in offensiveness in the towns, polluting drinking water and degrading the people.

Much has been written about the dreadfulness of the new manufacturing towns, and the squalor in which people lived. Manchester was described by Kay, London by Mayhew, and Engels gave a monumental picture in his *Condition of the Working Classes in England in 1844*.[3] Slavery, as we have seen, was accepted in older civilizations as necessary, and grinding poverty had always been part of the problems of all the cities of the world. The slum dweller aroused the pity and fear of the ruling classes so that a Vauban could advocate doing something about not ignoring the poor, while a Haussmann could cut fine new streets through the slums to help to control

[1] *The Decline of the West*, Vol. II, p. 412.
[2] The non-conformity and irreverence of this class is symbolized in the inscription of Dr. Young's grave in Belfast.
[3] See Bibliography.

their inhabitants. The nineteenth century, however, full of confidence in a new and glorious future made possible by progress, could produce hundreds of ideas full of faith and the desire to change things for the better. Outrage was to rise in the bosoms of radicals, churchmen, freethinkers and reformers alike, but such an emotion was only to stir the souls of the ruling classes after the public conscience had been severely jolted by several extremely nasty events in the course of the nineteenth century.

The first of these was the Peterloo massacre of 1819, when an unarmed crowd assembled to hear orator Hunt. The Magistrates, filled with fear at the size of the crowd, decided to have Hunt arrested, and when the soldiers attempted to do so, the people obstructed them. The cavalry was ordered in, and in the ensuing panic, eleven people were killed and hundreds were hurt. The sense of outrage which Peterloo bred was such that radicals like Cobbett and Bentham were heard, not as dangerous revolutionaries, but as genuine reformers. Cobbett's identification of the problems of the day with the attitudes of M.P.'s, the government, landowners, clergymen and capitalists was to have far-reaching results in that it crystallized future class antagonism, but, on a positive side, workers' associations, which had been banned in 1800 as a wartime measure, were permitted again in 1824.

The second shock to public conscience, accentuated by fear, was the outbreak of cholera epidemics in the 1830's and 1840's which forced legislation in sanitary matters, including sewage disposal, dumping, water supply, and the disposal of the dead. A report by the Poor Law Commissioners in 1838 on the epidemic in Whitechapel led to Chadwick's *Report on the Sanitary Conditions of the Labouring Population* of 1842. This report was responsible for later developments in legislation which created the Public Health Acts. In 1844 legislation was passed in which minimum sanitary requirements were defined; the use of cellars for human habitation was prohibited and public baths were to be provided. This applied only to London, but further outbreaks of cholera hastened the passing of the *Public Health Act* of 1848. This Act brought in requirements for sewerage to be managed by the Boards of Health; provision for refuse collection and disposal; action to be taken in the case of a danger to health; the inspection of places where animals were killed; the inspection of lodging houses; paving of roads; provision and maintenance of public gardens; water supply; and disposal of the dead. Such Acts as the Towns Improvement Clauses Act, the

Town Police Clauses Act, and the Waterworks, Gasworks, Cemeteries and Markets and Fairs Clauses Acts had been passed in 1847, but they were of limited application, whereas the Public Health Act was a comprehensive enactment giving new powers to local authorities which were to be consolidated and increased by the Act of 1875.

With regard to the burial of the dead, it is interesting to note that as early as the seventeenth century, John Evelyn had campaigned for the formation of cemeteries outside the City after the Plague and Fire of 1665 and 1666. By the beginning of the nineteenth century, the state of the churchyards was disgusting. Abuses extended to chapels being erected as speculative enterprises, the cellars of which were used for burials. Enon Chapel, off the Strand, was built in 1823, and the upper part, which was used for worship, was separated from the lower by a boarded floor. In the vault, 12,000 bodies were interred.[1] Quicklime was used to hasten the destruction of the flesh, and the coffins were removed and burnt. Agitation for burial reform increased after the cholera epidemics, which produced chaos in the already choked churchyards. G. F. Garden, in the *Penny Magazine*, had agitated for reform for years, and between 1835 and 1855 attention was drawn in the press and in parliament to the state of affairs. In 1842 a committee of the House of Commons was appointed to study the problem. The various Burial Acts stopped intramural interments, expressly excluding St. Paul's Cathedral and Westminster Abbey. The first innovation, despite the opposition of the clergy, was the founding of great cemeteries outside the towns, Kensal Green being formed in 1832, closely followed by many others including Highgate in 1839. These private enterprise cemeteries were followed, after the setting up of Committees of Health in 1847, by properly enclosed local authority cemeteries. Many of these nineteenth century cemeteries made a positive contribution to the Victorian towns and cities both architecturally and from the point of view of landscaping. Eclecticism was rampant, of course, Kensal Green being notable for its splendid Greek Revival propylaea and chapel, while Highgate has Egyptian Revival, Gothick vaults and a chapel, as well as the most lush and Italianate landscaping.[2] The Burial Acts also recognized

---

[1] *London* pp. 161–176.
[2] See *The History and Antiquities of Highgate*, and *The History, Topography and Antiquities of Highgate*. (See Bibliography.)

that the old burial grounds could become valuable assets in towns, and churchwardens were empowered to plant shrubs and trees.[1]

The third event which shook the conscience of Victorian England was the series of hideous murders in London in the autumn of 1888. The melodramatic nature of these crimes horrified the whole of society from the Queen to the lowest drabs of Whitechapel. The East End of London had originally developed as a series of villages associated with various trades, notably the Huguenot weavers of Spitalfields and Bethnal Green. The cottage industries had declined, and the prosperous had moved out to new suburbs, leaving the older areas to decay, so that by the 1870's and 1880's, the beautiful eighteenth century streets had become the most appalling slums inhabited by all the dregs of the London underworld. By the early eighteenth century, Spitalfields, Bethnal Green, Stepney Green and Stoke Newington had fine streets of houses and magnificent churches by architects such as Hawksmoor. Some of these villages forming the East End had ancient origins: Stepney was a Saxon village. As the City became less populated with the expansion of business and commercial premises, so pressures grew on the inner rings of suburbs. With the decline in cottage industries and the exodus to suburbia by the middle classes, such areas became gradually more run down and poor in character. The growth of industry and dockland activity along the river amalgamated the hamlets, and successive waves of immigrants from the pogroms of Poland and Russia gave it the amazingly diverse character that it still possesses, with a strong Jewish influence expressed in the Sunday markets, kosher restaurants and shops, synagogues and Jewish schools.

By 1888, Dorset Street, Spitalfields, under the shadow of Hawksmoor's great Christ Church, whose churchyard was known as 'itchy park' from the large numbers of down and outs who slept there, was noted as the most evil street in the metropolis. When two Whitechapel alcoholic whores who lodged in this street were disembowelled nothing much happened at first, as such events were not uncommon. When, however, the perpetrator wrote to the newspapers, to the police and to the authorities informing them that he was going to continue his slaughter, the excitement quickened, and when he actually murdered two more prostitutes on the same night, one of them in the City of London, as he had promised, the sense of outrage was complete. The murderer then wrote announcing he

[1] *London* pp. 161–176.

had eaten half of one of the kidneys of his last victim for breakfast, and enclosed the other half to prove it. He then spiced his boast with humorous poetry on the speculation as to his identity, and the scene was ripe for violence, as it was rumoured he was Jewish, or Russian, or Polish, possibly a doctor, perhaps a barber, and so on. The groups in the multiracial population viewed other groups with suspicion: certainly, it was firmly decided, the murderer could not be an Englishman. The legend of Jack the Ripper was born. Agitation grew to a tremendous pitch to improve the lot of the poor, and the East End became a subject for reformers. Earlier, Mayhew had drawn attention to the vile conditions under which the urban poor lived, conditions of which patently the upper classes were oblivious.[1] The Peabody Trust and the Improved Industrial Dwellings Company had provided some model dwellings for the poor, but these attempts were very small-scale. William Booth had done valuable work with his Salvation Army, but society was not really touched to the point of legislating radically.

This could have continued indefinitely had not Jack the Ripper struck again, leaving behind him a masterpiece in ghastliness. In a room in Miller's Court, off Dorset Street (renamed Duval Street after the murder) he killed an Irish tart named Mary Kelly, or Marie Kelly, and cut her to pieces, arranging her entrails in artistic designs all over the walls, bed and table. The police photographed the room completely, and the newspapers gave the story national publicity, sparing none of the details, as the Victorian newspapers were much less squeamish about such matters than are our own papers of today. The shudder of horror which greeted this latest crime really began public intervention in housing in poorer districts in earnest, for the political climate created by the outraged public conscience helped the passing of the *Housing of the Working Classes Act, 1890*, which marked the first stage in housing law on a modern scale, providing for slum clearance and the supply of new houses for the working classes. This act subsequently culminated in the *Housing Act* of 1925, and in later Acts up to the present day.

The Public Health Act of 1875 was directly responsible for the appearance of huge areas of late nineteenth century towns, for it laid down minimum requirements and by-law regulations with respect to new buildings and future streets. The power given to local authorities in this Act was a precedent for much later legisla-

[1] See *London's Underworld* by Henry Mayhew.

tion, but its immediate effect was that development after 1875 had a depressing regularity and soul-less regimentation due to the slavish following of the minimal dimensional requirements of the by-laws. This tendency has not lessened with the years, minimal ministry requirements being adhered to as criteria in housing of our own day.

Nineteenth century towns acquired large numbers of churches. After the Napoleonic Wars, it was seen that many new churches were needed, and in 1818 a Church Building Society was founded, and an Act of Parliament appointed Commissioners who were responsible for the building of two hundred or more churches, many in London and the industrial towns. Eminent architects, such as Nash and Soane, designed churches for the Commissioners, and many of these were in the Gothic style. Classicism, however, persisted in the public buildings, such as the National Gallery and the British Museum. Antiquated boundaries of parishes and dioceses created the situations where many churches were successful, while others were never full, even in the pious Victorian age. Many decaying nineteenth century churches adorn our towns today, some of which have always been superfluous.

Towns also acquired a significant addition to the streetscape in the nineteenth century in the form of the gin palace. Much nonsense has been written about this splendid institution, attributing to it unimaginable evils. To put the record straight we must return to eighteenth century times, where, contemplating the moralistic works of Hogarth, we can only be aware that the consumption of cheap gin was a great social problem even then. In Ireland, drunkenness was a national failing, and probably the only escape-route from abject misery.[1] Parliamentary action, aided by the temperance lobby, aimed to check the consumption of cheap gin by an act of 1869 which permitted the sale of beer in unlicensed premises. The small beer-houses which mushroomed as a result were a threat to the large breweries, so the brewers commenced the purchase of pubs and the building of new ones, usually at corner sites in streets. This process has resulted in a monopoly for the great brewers of today. The licensed houses were permitted to sell spirits, and the public was attracted in by the ornate and comfortable décor of these 'gin palaces' which were the result of the evils of drink and not their cause. An interesting influence on *Hygeia*, a Utopia

[1] See the last part of *National Evils and Practical Remedies* pp. 483–512.

planned by B. W. Richardson, was the use in the gin palaces of *Lincrusta* and glazed tiles, which substances Richardson recommended as wall and ceiling coverings.[1]

State intervention had had some precedents in the 1840's when options for state purchase of the railways were mooted, and a standard gauge was laid down by law, together with regulations as to speed, times and prices. Procedure for the acquisition of land was regulated in the '40's.

The 1832 Reform Bill began a series of enactments which created the workhouses and eased the way for such reformers as Chadwick (1800–1890) and the Earl of Shaftesbury (1801–1885). Chadwick we have already mentioned in connection with public health; but Shaftesbury was responsible for many social improvements, among which may be mentioned the forming of the 'Ragged Schools,' the Y.M.C.A., Working Men's Institutes and the Ten Hours Bill.

UTOPIAS OF THE NINETEENTH CENTURY

In 1783, David Dale met Arkwright the inventor, and the partnership which they formed in order to erect cotton spinning mills found expression at New Lanark on the Clyde. This industrial village, begun in 1784, incorporated much of the humane ideology of David Dale, and when he sold it in 1799 to his son-in-law, Robert Owen, it was already a thriving concern. Owen was a member of the Literary and Philosophical Society of Manchester, one of many such societies which proliferated at the beginning of the nineteenth century, with a membership largely drawn from non-conformist and radical members of the new middle class. Owen knew many members who had advanced opinions, many of which were regarded as subversive during the anti-Jacobin feeling of the wars, and he developed his theories as to the importance of providing a decent environment for workers. A reasonable length of working week; good, spacious dry housing; fair pay and social services for the community were among Owen's innovations. A nursery was established for children so that the parents could work, and schools were founded to teach not only the rudiments of education, but the social graces as well. These ideas were expressed in the Institution for the Formation of Character (1812) and the New Institution (1816) which had heating by means of warm air.[2] The village shop

[1] See *A Prospect of Cities* p. 169.
[2] *New Lanark*. See Bibliography.

was on co-operative lines, and goods of quality were sold, ensuring that the pay packet would not be squandered. Family fortunes were also preserved by the absence of pubs. There was no church as such, but part of an upper floor in the New Building was used for services, reflecting Owen's anti-establishment views on religion.

Robert Owen put forward his ideas in a *Report concerning the Relief of the Manufacturing Poor*, advocating a national application of his methods. His 'Villages of Co-operation' were intended as a beginning of nothing less than the complete change of the industrial structure. Significantly, the plans Owen produced for his villages showed a variant of the mandala pattern on a parallelogram basis, containing all the services, work facilities and residential areas necessary for life. Education, work, health and social improvement were to be part and parcel of the scheme, but with the regulating plan came a regulating notion: children, for example, were to be segregated from their parents to avoid their acquiring 'bad habits from their parents'. After the Napoleonic Wars, however, Owen came out openly against established religions, and in the prevailing political climate became regarded as a dangerous radical and a devil's advocate. His book[1] expressed much of his vision of the future, but in a Zeitgeist which was 'return to normal and stay that way', his views went largely unheeded. Owen subsequently emigrated to America where he attempted to found new societies at New Harmony, Indiana, Yellow Springs, Cincinnati, and Mashoba, Tennessee, all of which had short-lived successes because the necessary mixture of trades and skills was not possessed by the settlers.[2]

New Harmony had its origins in a foundation by George Rapp, a German reformer. It was a gridiron plan, with a central square. After unsuccessful approaches to the president of the U.S.A. and to the authorities in Mexico, Owen returned to England, where he became leader of the co-operative movement and agitator for reforms in the economy and in society. Owen's ideas were seriously considered by the growing trade unions and co-op. societies, and a community based on his theories existed for a few years at Queenswood, Hants. After the 1848 disturbances throughout western society, socialism began to develop as a force, but the political climate was one of 'reformist conservatism',[3] and Owen's ideas be-

[1]   *A New View of Society.*
[2]   *A Prospect of Cities* pp. 146–147.
[3]   *The Origins of Modern Town Planning* pp. 53–54.

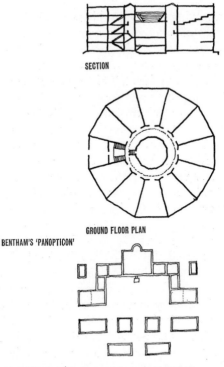

SECTION

GROUND FLOOR PLAN

BENTHAM'S 'PANOPTICON'

FOURIER'S 'PHALANSTÈRE' [interior streets shown as double lines]

Panopticon and Phalanstère   Figure No. 28

came watered down into purely economic consideration, divorced from physical planning.

Of interest in Utopian terms is Jeremy Bentham who was born in 1748. His *Fragment on Government, Principles of Morals and Legislation, Defence of Usury, Emancipate your Colonies* and *Chrestomathia* expressed much of his opinion. His influence on practical reform was enormous, and the Reform Bill owed a great deal to his ideas. His influence on the continent was significant, and in France he was known as Le Grand Bentham.[1] He propounded the philosophy of utilitarianism, being the creation of the greatest happiness for the greatest number of people, and his *Panopticon*, an 'Industry-House Establishment for 2,000 Persons of All Ages' was developed from this concept. It was really a prison, but it incorporated the advanced technique of constructional methods of the day with

[1] Article by A. P. Ryan in *The Times*, 15:2:1968.

idealism for improving society, in this case, criminals. Significantly, the plan of the *Panopticon* was a polygonal mandala shape.

Pugin's *Contrasts*[1] was an important publication since he denounced the towns and society of his own day and painted a picture of a 'Catholic City' as an ideal. This Gothic Revivalist had a great influence on later developments especially after Catholic Emancipation (1829) and the reforms of the '30's. The Gothic Revival, which had been mooted in work by Wren and Hawksmoor and certainly kept simmering as an image in poetry and literature, really began with Horace Walpole's *Castle of Otranto* and Strawberry Hill. A cultivated ruling and fashionable class took up Gothic things with great enthusiasm. Soane, Adam, Wyatt, Chambers and Nash all carried out exercises in Gothic, until it became utterly respectable and not merely a fashion. The Church Building Act of 1818 was responsible for a great number of Gothic churches, but it was Pugin who put the seal of piety on Gothic Revivalism. Gothic was taken up with enthusiasm by Anglicans too, who were developing their own High Church Party, and the Tractarians and the Camden Society adopted Gothic as their own style. The result, in a Zeitgeist of intense religious revival was a mushrooming of Victorian Gothic throughout the land, and soon even railway stations were built in Gothic, as well as town halls, schools and universities. One or two gin palaces became gothicized. The influence of John Ruskin was very strong, especially after the publication of his *Seven Lamps of Architecture* (1849) and *The Stones of Venice* (1851–1853). For Ruskin, art and architecture were moral issues, and his emphasis on the beauties of Gothic and the nature of craftsmanship helped to create a Zeitgeist wherein solidly and beautifully constructed and detailed Gothic Revival architecture proliferated.

In France, industrial development and urbanization did not really begin until some 50 years after England, and French towns continued to express a traditional political climate, due to the restoration of the Bourbon Monarchy and the perpetuation of the old régime. Under the Orleans monarchy of Louis-Philippe, Napoleonic monuments were completed and even the emperor's body was brought back from St. Helena for a hero's funeral under the dome of the Invalides, a significant resting place as the centre of a mandala, later developed when the Unknown Soldier was buried in the centre of the larger rond-point mandala under the Arc de

[1] See Bibliography.

Plate 85 : The portico of St. George's Church, Belfast.

Plate 86 : The curious atmosphere of Anglo-Irish towns is epitomised at Downpatrick.
To the left is the Southwell School; to the right is the prison; and dominating the
town is the cathedral of St. Patrick, seat of the Protestant Bishop.

Plate 87: St. Mary's Church, Belfast.

Plate 88: 19th century eclecticism. Church and houses are
approximately contemporary (mid 19th Cent.), Belfast.

Plate 89: The Protestant Cathedral from the Roman Catholic one opposite. Armagh.

Plate 90: Caledon.

Plate 91 : Liverpool Street Station.

Plate 92: Factory at Hilden, Co. Antrim. A good example of enlightened factory architecture.

Plate 93: *19th century industrial scene. It could be one of many places, but it is in fact Belfast. A contrast with Hilden.*

Plate 94: *Unfortunately the backs of the Hilden houses are left to look after themselves.*

Plate 95: Working class Housing in Belfast. Despite the fact that these houses are absolutely minimal, they are brightly painted and clean.

Plate 96: Dr. Young's grave in the old cemetery, Belfast.

Plate 97 : Highgate Cemetery.
(From an article by the author in the R.I.B.A. Journal of April 1968.)

Plate 98: Christ Church, Spitalfields.

Plate 99: St. Katherine's Docks, London.

Plate 100: Typical working class housing in Whitechapel.
Jack the Ripper's first victim was killed here.

Plate 101: Four per cent industrial dwellings in the East End. (1889–90)

Plate 102: Four per cent industrial dwellings in the East End. (1889–90)

Plate 103: The Gin Palace. The Crown Liquor Saloon, Belfast.
(*Published in* Country Life *and in* Bauwelt *in 1969.*)

Plate 104: The Gin Palace. The Crown Liquor Saloon, Belfast.
(*Published in* Country Life *and in* Bauwelt *in 1969.*)

Plate 105: The Gin Palace. The Crown Liquor Saloon, Belfast.
(*Published in* Country Life *and in* Bauwelt *in 1969.*)

Plate 106: Pub in William IV St., London.
(*First published in the* Journal *of the* R.I.B.A. *1969.*)

Plate 107: Strawberry Hill.

Plate 108: Strawberry Hill.

Plate 109: Balliol, Oxford.

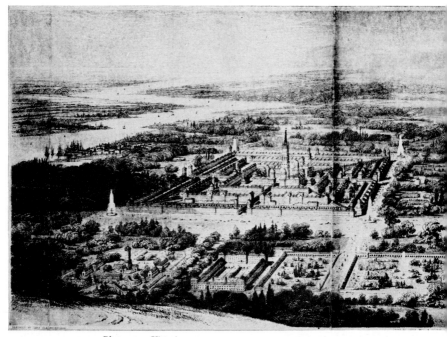

Plate 110: Victoria. (From National Evils and Practical Remedies.*)*

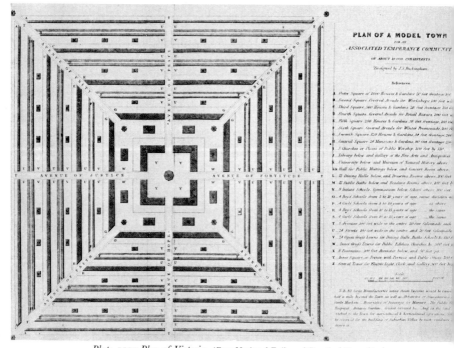

Plate 111: Plan of Victoria. (From National Evils and Practical Remedies.*)*

Plate 112: Siegfried Allee, Bayreuth.

Plate 113: The Burg-garten, Vienna.

Plate 114: The New Hofburg, Vienna, G. Semper, Architect.

Plate 115: The dominance of 19th century commerce. The Ulster Bank, Belfast. A fine example of Victorian classicism.

Triomphe. The concept of a military and popular world domination had great potency at the time, and the Orleans monarchy pandered to it. At the same time English Utopian ideas were filtering into France and gaining ground. Bentham we have already mentioned as being regarded as a sage by the French.

Saint-Simon[1] proposed that technicians and workers should hold power instead of the existing classes, and after the 1830 Revolution, his ideas were expounded by disciples. A plan for Paris appeared in 1832, and large scale operations were proposed with emphasis on the moral value of public works.

Fourier (1772–1837) in his publications promulgated ideas about his specific Utopia in which a harmony between the interests of rich and poor based on association would be reached after seven historic periods had been gone through.[2] Physically, Fourier expressed his ideas in plans for a *Phalanstère* published in *Le Nouveau Monde*.[3] This was a highly organized plan, formal, with strong axes reminiscent of baroque planning, and, within the *Phalanstère*, workshops, dining halls, finance halls, libraries, study rooms, residential quarters and community halls were to be provided. Essentially, it was a town minus open streets, enclosed, heated and ventilated, the noisier parts being connected with the centre or cité by means of covered arcades. The denizens of the *Phalanstère* were to be members with accommodation and shares, and forced equality was to be avoided since variety would be aimed at by the different qualities of the people, their occupations and abilities. The baroque plan was echoed in the covered arcades and elevations of the scheme.

J. B. Godin and others attempted to put the ideas of Fourier into practice, and some successes were recorded in America. Godin's *Familistère* of 1859–1877 was an expression of Fourier-type ideas first published in *Solutions Sociales* in 1870. While Fourier envisaged communal living and an economy based on horticulture and agriculture, helped by industry, Godin developed the industrial basis of an economy, abandoning the communal ideas, except for the use of open land. The *Familistère* was built as a unit in which the buildings were not scattered but embraced many functions including educational facilities, so that the rest of the land could be used as an open park. Godin also adopted the covered street idea of

[1] Le Comte de Saint-Simon (1760–1825).
[2] *The Ideal City* p. 134, and *The Origins of Modern Town Planning* pp. 56 and 57.
[3] Paris, 1829.

Fourier in the great covered courtyards of the residential blocks. In 1880, the whole complex which had been at Guise was handed over to a workers' co-operative as a self-sufficient going concern. Another Frenchman, Cabét, founded a communal town based on ideas in a novel by him, at Nauvoo, in Illinois. Cabét propounded communism, but argument, not violence, was to accomplish the millennium. He had met Owen, and no doubt developed many of his own concepts from Owenite originals. Later, his followers founded Icaria in 1860, which was square in plan, the centre of which had a large open space (as at Freudenstadt) with communal buildings grouped round it. The communal puritanical and idealistic nature of these socialistic Utopias was similar to that of nonconformist settlements in the nineteenth century. Rappite villages at Harmony and Economy;[1] German towns at Amana, Zoar and Bethel; Norwegian ones at New Bergen and Valhalla; and Mormon settlements at Nauvoo and Salt Lake City all had much in common with socialistic foundations.

Robert Owen influenced many subsequent developments, but we must not forget the influence that writers of novels had on public conscience. Charles Dickens and Benjamin Disraeli[2] painted vivid pictures of life at the time, and the political climate of the 1840's may have been profoundly influenced by their work as well as by the cholera epidemics and by famine in Ireland. Experiments in housing took place in England at the time and a Society for Improving the Dwellings of the Labouring Classes was formed. We have mentioned the work of John Grubb Richardson at Bessbrook, Ulster, in 1846, and Benjamin Ward Richardson's *Hygeia*.[3]

Another influential work was *National Evils and Practical Remedies with the Plan of a Model Town* by James S. Buckingham. Buckingham had attacked slavery and suggested practical methods of freeing all slaves in an article in the *Oriental Herald* for March, 1825. Earlier, in 1818, writing in the *Calcutta Journal* he proposed the development of the Suez route to India, and he was an advocate, while in India from 1818–1823, of many reforms which were later carried out. In his 1849 publication, he takes the temperance line, advocating

[1]   See *National Evils and Practical Remedies* pp. 260–270.
[2]   See *Sybil, or The Two Nations*.
[3]   Another *Hygeia* had been proposed in 1827 by John Buonarroti Papworth, Architect of the King of Württemberg, for a site on the Ohio River. The plan had a central mandala form of square and circle with radiating roads. Houses were detached, with separate gardens.

Health and Exercise, Serenity of Mind, Competency of Means, Labour in a Moderate degree, Progressive Advancement, and Love and Respect. The stunting and degradation of people he regarded as 'arising from architectural and municipal defects alone' while intemperance comes in for a round denunciation. Buckingham's model town, named *Victoria*, was unlike the smaller Utopian solutions in that it was urban in scale, uniting 'the greatest degree of order, symmetry, space, and healthfulness . . . with the comfort and convenience of all classes . . .'. 'Shelter from sun and rain, where necessary', was to be provided, while 'the whole' was 'to be united with as much elegance and economy as may be found practicable.'[1] The town of Victoria is described in some detail.[2] It was to be a mandala shape, square, with eight avenues radiating from a central square in which was a 'Central Tower for Electric Light, Clock and Gallery, 300 feet high'. The outer square of 1,000 houses and gardens of 20 foot frontage and a depth of 100 feet was to house workers. The second square in was a covered arcade 'of the Gothic order' for workshops 100 feet wide,[3] while the third square had 560 houses and gardens of 28 foot frontage and 130 foot depth. The fourth square was a covered arcade 'like the Burlington Arcade' for 'retail bazars' (*sic*). The fifth was a square of houses and gardens of a more salubrious nature for the professional classes, while the sixth was a 'Covered Arcade for Winter Promenade, 100 feet wide' which was to be enriched with paintings and statuary. The seventh square was one of superior houses for the wealthy, while the central square had '24 mansions and Gardens'. Between the mansions and square number seven were 5 churches, a library, a gallery, a university, a museum, a hall and a concert room. Mixed with the residential areas were to be dining halls, public baths, reading rooms, schools, gymnasia, fountains, lawns and 'public buildings'. All offensive manufactories, abattoirs, markets, cemeteries and noisy activities were to be removed half a mile beyond the town, which was described as being for an 'Associated Temperance Community of about 10,000 inhabitants'. Buckingham's *Victoria* was a splendid

---

[1] *National Evils and Practical Remedies* p. 183.
[2] *Ibid.* pp. 183–199.
[3] On p. 184 'a colonnade of the light Gothic order' is mentioned. On p. 186 the *Gothic* order is referred to, while the *Ionic, Corinthian* and *composite* orders are brought in on pp. 188, 189 and 190. Therefore, it would seem that the reference on p. 186 should read '*Doric* order', for Buckingham clearly considered that the orders of architecture consisted of the Gothic, Doric, Ionic, Corinthian and composite types (p. 190).

conception and could only have been designed by an individual confident of his own rightness. The Utopian ideal is symbolized in the mandala form, and the perspective of *Victoria*, designed by Buckingham and drawn by James Bell and George Childs, shows many features of interest. In the foreground are the cemeteries, influenced no doubt by Highgate and Kensal Green; a large factory; and what might be pleasure gardens. The town itself is depicted as having covered galleries, influenced, probably, by the *Phalanstère*,[1] and modern techniques of iron construction were recommended.[2]

Mr. Buckingham then continues to expound[3] on the attention to houses by 'Mr. Laycock of Liverpool', and to a pamphlet by Mr. Alexander Gordon. Both these references pre-date *Cast Iron Buildings* by James Bogardus (1856). Paxton's Crystal Palace of 1851 was a remarkable achievement using cast iron, and looked forward to future developments, but the Great Exhibition was also notable for the erection of model dwellings in Hyde Park by Prince Albert.

In 1853, Sir Titus Salt began Saltaire, which is wonderfully described by Cecil Stewart.[4] According to Stewart, Salt was inspired to build a model factory of great magnificence as well as a model village after reading *Sybil*. His village incorporates much of Owen's reforming ideas, but the political climate of the 1850's ensured prolific church building, so that all sects were amply catered for. 'Boozers' were out, however, for Salt, like many of his fellow reformers, was an ardent temperance supporter.[5]

Other settlements followed, among them the Cadbury village of Bournville, which laid down in a trust deed the relationship of houses to open space, and did not specifically exist for the workers in the factories. The first house was erected in 1879, and extremely spacious layouts were created. In 1888, W. H. Lever (later Lord Leverhulme) moved his works to a new site near Birkenhead, also founding a colony for the workers built out of the profits they themselves created. As an example of property sharing it is a direct descendant of early nineteenth century ideas. Both Port Sunlight and Bournville were low density developments centred on the

---

[1] Buckingham mentions Fourier, Owen, Saint-Simon, Cabét and Louis Blanc on p. 246.
[2] p. 195.
[3] pp. 195–196.
[4] *A Prospect of Cities* Chapter 8. pp. 148–167.
[5] Apart from *Saltaire and its Founder* by Holroyd, this chapter in *A Prospect of Cities* remains the most valuable as well as the most readable and entertaining essay on Salt that the present writer has found.

works, but they both achieved spectacular results in improved health of the inhabitants.

Other industrialists founded model settlements. In the 1860's and 1870's, the Krupps built many such developments near Essen, and several European experiments followed. In England, the work of Ebenezer Howard has become famous. He rationalized the Utopian ideas and equated them with successful developments, drawing attention to the problems of the '90's such as rural depopulation and the overcrowding in cities.[1] Essentially, his ideas were to take the best of town and country and to mingle them in a 'garden city' where all the advantages of town and country would be found without the problems. Among the evils of the town were gin palaces, according to Howard, showing he did not understand the nature of such places, due to his own religious and ethical code. Howard's diagrams are circular in form, and he adopted mandala shapes for his 'garden city' with radiating boulevards from a central point round which would be grouped the hospital, library, theatre, concert hall, town hall, museum and gallery. This cultural, municipal and curative ghetto was to be separated by a large park from the rest of the town, an idea that has been perpetuated ever since in the cold 'civic centres' of so many projects and towns. The separation of 'culture' and 'civic buildings' from the organic whole of the town is a symbol of our age, and was described by Rilke in his 'Sorrow-Town', with its concepts formed in 'a mould of vacuity'. Rilke describes such a centre as being 'as tidy and disappointed and shut' as a Post Office on a Sunday. On the circumference of Howard's town were the factories and railway system. However, to be fair, the diagrams in his book were only diagrammatic, but the idea of separation is still there, plainly for all to see. The result of these ideas was the formation of First Garden City Ltd., which began to lay out Letchworth after 1903 on a non-regular pattern. Many concepts such as the creation of a green belt; control of the planning by one body; a diversity of industry zoned to avoid nuisance; and the adoption of a low density to get the benefits of Bournville and Port Sunlight with regard to health were incorporated in Letchworth. The diversity of industry made sure the Garden City was viable economically. Dr. Rosenau suggests[2] that Howard may have been influenced by Pemberton's *Happy Colony*, which was a mandala circle with eight radiating roads dividing the

[1] *Garden Cities of Tomorrow.*
[2] *The Ideal City* p. 142.

plan into segments. The three layouts, Letchworth, Welwyn and Hampstead Garden Suburb were all supposed to be descendants of Howard's ideas. The last can be discounted, as the only connection it has with *Garden Cities of Tomorrow* is the fact that it had the same architects as Letchworth, and that it was a low density open development, with lots of garden-space. Garden cities were supposed to be cities, and Howard advocated that town life and country life should intermingle; that work should be near homes; and that the importance of agriculture to the city must be borne in mind. Howard's 'garden city' was to be a satellite of the city in whose service area it was situated, and further growth would be in the form of further satellite towns, each with a green belt, until finally the parent town would be ringed with satellites, an idea which found expression in the post-war New Towns. *It must be emphasized that the naming of speculative housing estates as 'garden cities' just because they were large and had gardens is not what Howard meant by the term.*

OTHER DEVELOPMENTS

A most interesting remodelling of an ancient city took place at Newcastle-upon-Tyne when the municipality, private enterprise and a talented local architect combined forces to replace the centre of the city. John Clayton (1792–1890) was Town Clerk of the city from 1822–1867, and his support for the speculator Richard Grainger (1797–1861) and the architect John Dobson (1787–1865) served to transform Newcastle from a somewhat run-down mediaeval town into a fine example of Victorian Classicism. Newcastle is blessed with a magnificent site, dominated by the lantern spire of the Cathedral of St. Nicholas. It is fortunate for the city that the splendid developments by the trio mentioned above took place at a time when the traditions of classicism and craftsmanship were still very much alive. The centre of Newcastle owes much to eighteenth century architecture and to Nash, especially Grainger Street and Grey Street. Traditions of progress and nonconformist intellectual activity were strong in Newcastle, and it possessed (and still does possess) a thriving Literary and Philosophical Society housed in a fine building by John Green the Elder. The spirit of progress and reform may be seen in the two remarkable buildings in Newcastle: the Central Station by Dobson; and the dominant column to Earl Grey, celebrating the Great Reformer.[1]

[1] See *Tyneside Classical* and *Newcastle upon Tyne, Its Growth and Achievement*.

The growth of transport was a major factor in the design of towns as well as in the reasons for their existence. Many towns were 'railway towns', such as Crewe and Didcot, while others, such as Swindon and Peterborough, had their characters completely changed by the coming of the railways. Stamford, in Lincolnshire, was to have been a railway town, but the Marquess of Exeter, the local landowner, resisted the scheme, so Peterborough was developed instead. The result is that Stamford preserves its original character while Peterborough has lost most of its quality.

The railways were also responsible for the development of the suburbs, for quick travel to work made the possibility of living outside the towns more alluring and within the grasp of the middle classes. As the cities became more densely built up, so the smoke and grime from millions of chimneys made places like London very disagreeable in foggy weather. Middle class areas such as the inner ring of suburbs were emptied as the suburbs developed, and the property vacated thus became working class housing, usually let as apartments, since the properties were large and intended for families and servants. Villas and semi-detached villas sprang up all round the towns, expressing in a variety of architectural fashions the confused values of a people suddenly given the means to live a watered-down version of the Romantic 'house in the country'. The house often expresses much about its inhabitants. A rich Victorian could choose his style and then ask his architect to provide him with the house of his fancy. Fonthill and Strawberry Hill were the ancestors of the Victorian villa, odd though it may seem, for what had at first been a style of rich eccentric noblemen with bizarre tastes now had become a moral style, or a 'Christian' style. The influence of Nash is obvious in Victorian Kensington, St. John's Wood or even Paddington, but by the time Hampstead, Highgate and Holloway were ripe for development as public transport enabled people to travel, Gothic villas were springing up. Romanticism, Christianity, Puritanism, and anti-eighteenth century feeling combined, helped by Ruskin, to produce the curious revivalist villas that can be formed outside any prosperous nineteenth century town. Again, it was an aberration of Ruskin's ideas that produced these curiosities, but it is the *interpretation* of an idea rather than the idea itself which always counts.

The development of horse trams, steam trams, and later, electric trams was responsible for a linear development out of the cities in a star-pattern, with residential areas within walking distances of the main lines of communication. Commercial and communal under-takings of diverse character lined the main routes where they could be serviced and also could be within easy reach of the people. Often, wedges of greenery lay between the main routes. An essential feature of the nineteenth century street was its diversified use: bookshops jostled with chemist, grocer, butcher, undertaker, religious trac-tarian, and numerous other enterprises, as well as being lived in. Corners were enlivened by the classic pub, a fantasy of etched glass, mahogany, gilt and ceramics. Churches were never far away, and catered for all shades and versions of Christianity, from Anglo-Catholicism to the Salvation Army. In central districts, offices, banks and premises of the great commercial interests were domi-nants in the streetscape. The growth of professionalism and insti-tutionalism was symbolized in the proud buildings of the learned societies, the courts, the clubs and the institutions. The confidence of the age and its technical prowess was symbolized in the great sewer systems, underground railways, main line termini and water towers, gasworks and docks. The commercial prowess and self-con-fidence of the Victorians is admirably expressed in the riverside architecture of London: the great warehouses and wharfs, cranes and offices, ships and jetties. There is a strange beauty in the dock-land parts of great cities which are worth a lot more consideration than they get. They express the fact that so much of Victorian wealth was built on trade and mastery of the sea routes.

In Europe, in Vienna, the city, like many other towns, remained in its expensive and massive baroque fortifications until half-way through the nineteenth century. This meant that living habits con-tinued to be centred on apartments and major European metro-politan centres continued to build high and densely as a result of the existence of fortifications which symbolized the unsettled politi-cal climate of former days. In England, city walls had disappeared much earlier, and there were never the monstrous constructions of Vienna, Paris and Berlin, because the existence of the nation-state and the geographical separation of the British Isles from the Euro-pean land-mass ensured the security of the towns. The removal of the fortifications became an opportunity for the grand expression of civic dignity and imperial pomp as in Vienna. The Hapsburgs had achieved a new lease of power as Austrian emperors since they had lost the Holy Roman Empire in 1806. The establishment of the Dual Monarchy, designed to get over any restiveness on the part of the Hungarians, had twin capitals, two thrones and two parlia-

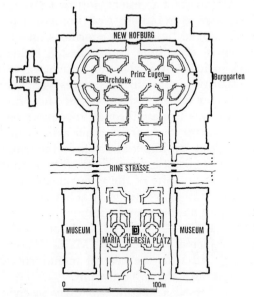

SCHEME BY SEMPER AND HASENAUER FOR THE NEW HOFBURG

Vienna   Figure No. 29

ments, nevertheless the imperial throne was in baroque Vienna. The character of the city was one of eighteenth century elegance, and examples of sumptuous layouts existed at the Schwarzenberg, the Belvedere and Schönbrunn. After 1857, the Ringstrasse was laid out on the lines of the old fortifications as a splendid boulevard, lined with the baroque device of the *Allee*, or regimented lines of trees, which Camillo Sitte roundly condemned.[1] The Ring was lined with important buildings: the Schottenring had the Stock Exchange; the Franzenring had the Rathaus, University, Burgtheater and Parliament; the Burgring passed the two major museums, the Hofburg, Hofgarten and Hofburgplatz; the remaining Opernring, Kärntnerring and Stubenring were enriched with the Opera House, Stadtpark, museums, War Ministry and Radetsky monument. In short, the Ring became a magnificent display piece for all the significant buildings that could be fitted in along

[1] In *City Planning according to Artistic Principles* p. 184.

it. In the plan by the great architect Gottfried Semper,[1] the Burg-ring passed through a grandiose *platz* composed of the Maria Theresia Platz, flanked by the two enormous museums, and the Hofburgplatz itself, sometimes known as the Heldenplatz. The Hofburg, much enriched by Fischer von Erlach, was to be extended by Semper so that two great curved palaces were to embrace the *platz* with its statues of the Archduke Karl and Prince Eugen of Savoy. The Ring was to pass through two enormous triumphal arches as it entered the space from either side. Camillo Sitte de-scribed the project as 'an imperial forum in the truest sense' and that it would 'be of gigantic dimensions'. Sitte admired the plan greatly, saying that 'in spite of the unfavourable current trends, great and beautiful things are still to be achieved . . . (despite) . . . the lack of taste that has become the fashion . . .'.[2] Unfortunately, this scheme was only partly finished. Only one wing of the new Hofburg was completed, although the Maria Theresia Platz was constructed, enriched with the central monument to the great Kaiserin and flanked by the two museums.

Semper also proposed a magnificent essay in civic design for Dresden, the Saxon capital. This scheme was for the completion of the Zwinger, but was not carried out as planned. His first building in Dresden was the Opera House, and it was while there that he met Wagner who was conductor at the opera. Both men had to flee as a result of their activities prior to and during the 1848 Revolution, and Semper's later writings express few open political attitudes, although he was clearly aware of social problems.[3]

Other Rings, developed because of the removal of the fortifica-tions, included those of Hamburg, Leipzig, München, Breslau, Bremen, Hannover, Antwerp, Prague, Würzburg and others.

Camillo Sitte (1843–1903), in his writings, praised mediaeval towns and compared developments of his own day unfavourably with them. His analyses of various examples of civic design in all periods are of absorbing interest. For Sitte, 'artistic principles' were

[1] This remarkable architect designed Wellington's Funeral Car. (See *The Duke of Wellington's Funeral Car*.) He is also significant in that he was among the first to become aware of the schism between art and industry. In this, he was a forerunner of William Morris, but, unlike Morris, he did not become an active socialist.

[2] *City Planning according to Artistic Principles* p. 118.

[3] Semper is discussed in an article by L. D. Ettlinger in *The Architectural Review* Volume CXXXVI.

as important as the considerations of layout to solve purely technical problems. He was involved in his own arts and crafts movement[1] and so his work and concern coincide to a certain extent with those of Morris and may be seen as part of a general concern by intellectuals of the period for the future of their environment and of craftsmanship.

Generally, in Europe and America, in civic design, strong axial influences prevailed, all stemming from French neo-classicism and the baroque tradition, Berlin, Vienna, Paris and many other cities received much of their civic ornament in the nineteenth century.

Toni Garnier proposed, in his *Cité Industrielle* of 1901–1904, a basic linear-pattern of design, so that residential areas would not be used for through traffic, and the main arteries would be within easy reach of the people. An industrial zone was to be separated from the town. Earlier, in 1882, Don Arturo Soria y Mata had proposed *Ciudad Lineal*, a linear design based on a spine for transport. The origins of Garnier's scheme are many, but among them may be mentioned the concern for the dangers to residential areas by noxious industry and the need to plan a rational transport system. The importance of the *Cité Industrielle* was that it was one of the first attempts to plan for all aspects of a town, including industry and possible future uses, such as a speedway. It thus looked forward to technological advances, whereas the great civic design schemes of the nineteenth century prolonged concepts of civic magnificence based on baroque, romantic or neo-classical modes of expression. The strength of Garnier's work lies in his looking at the problem of the modern town as a whole, understanding the social and technical problems, avoiding specialized solutions or interests, and in producing a plan which tried to combine all the differing functions of the town within a rational physical expression. This approach is very different from the other essays of the nineteenth century which had specialized in this or that aspect. The road brigade had ploughed streets through various cities as a panacea to all ills (Shaftesbury Avenue is an example of this), while others had additional reasons for being created, such as backgrounds for display and the facilitation of the restoration of order (Haussmann's Paris). Many minds turned to the question of providing housing for the poorer classes, which problem produced a spate of legislation, rules and regulations. Other places had been ideals, but Garnier's plan

[1] *Camillo Sitte and the Birth of Modern City Planning* p. 11.

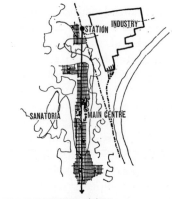

CITÉ INDUSTRIELLE BY TONI GARNIER [SKETCH]

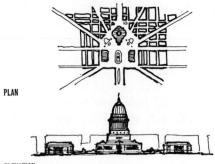

PLAN

ELEVATION
PROJECT FOR THE CHICAGO CIVIC CENTRE

Action and reaction   Figure No. 30

was the first to look forward, not backward to ancient forms. He sought to create a new environment, not an interpretation of older ideas to modern technological needs. Compared with other plans of the period, such as those for Chicago and Berlin which only selected specialized aspects such as traffic improvement, the addition of greenery, satellite settlements and grandiose neo-classical and neo-baroque civic centre schemes, the *Cité Industrielle* was far in advance of its time. Other schemes, however, such as Burnham and Bennett's Chicago Civic Centre reflect a political climate in which overblown civic pomposity was thought to express the progress and wealth of society. Many early twentieth century American schemes for town centres are amazing essays in monumental axial planning, with great civic magnificence. The realities of housing, industry and commercial wealth were expressed in the beginning of endless urban sprawl, in huge apartment blocks, in factory complexes and in the great 'skyscrapers' of commercial enterprises.

This curious state of affairs is directly related to the rise of professionalism and institutionalism, for architects were trained in a tradition which had little or no relationship with the social realities of the day. Dogmas, creeds and professional attitudes here developed which paid no heed to the broader view of the problems of city design. Professional dogma had been responsible for absurdities throughout the nineteenth century: during the cholera epidemic learned pamphlets were produced blaming cholera on everything from cucumber to fogs, while remedies included exploding gunpowder in the streets and burning tar-barrels. When it was suggested that perhaps cholera was caused by a living organism carried in drinking water, the medical profession was outraged. In earlier times the professional Inquisitors had built up complex beliefs and torture methods all founded on a revival of superstition. Later, the very ideas which in their day had been sound, such as Garnier's and Howard's concepts of industrial zoning, developed into the dogma of professionalism, and zoning, dividing human activities into compartments, became articles of faith. Many modern factories, emitting neither noise nor fumes are no more noxious than a school, yet they have to go in an industrial zone. Such attitudinizing is similar to the kind of political climate within the professions which produced the inflated absurdities of turn of the century civic design.

The 'skyscraper' had developed from Chicago in the '80's, in work by Richardson, Jenney, and Sullivan, but often, at the turn of the century, tower forms had been introduced with debased classical ornamentation. Later expressions of skyscrapers, however, are to Giedion 'as significant and expressive for our period as the monolithic obelisk of Egypt and the Gothic cathedral tower were for their periods'.[1] A new dominant had appeared: the enormously wealthy and powerful business corporation which expressed itself in the huge buildings of the late nineteenth and early twentieth centuries. The symbols of the huge commercial enterprises were to appear everywhere, until, as we shall see, they finally permeated the whole of our urban civilization.

---

[1] *Space, Time and Architecture* p. 750.

IX

Modern Times

THE MAIN DEVELOPMENTS IN BRITAIN

It is not my intention to discuss the details of planning law and the regulations which have led up to the present-day approaches to town design. A broader view will be taken.

Since the beginning of the century, and indeed ever since the 1875 'by-law' housing, the problem of providing dwellings has been based on minimum 'objective' standards, usually of a sanitary or a size nature. The term 'slum' has become a term of abuse, applied equally to housing which does not fit the pre-conceived notions of what is proper as well as to dwellings lacking basic amenities. Officially recognized slums correspond in number with the amount of housing a Government intends to demolish in a period of time plus an amount it has decided to clear later.[1] Housing is a political pawn, and a compilation of quantities, slum-clearance and numbers rehoused is used on the political scoreboard to convey the excellence of this or that party. The statistics and figures are one thing, being mistaken for reality, but the truth is different, for the quality of environment in housing is dismal indeed.

Significantly, many model dwellings of the nineteenth century have been among the most recent of demolitions, and there is a very good reason for this: they represented officialdom, and as such were subjected to harsh treatment by the tenants. Modern housing schemes are products of an expanded officialdom, and they incorporate much that is already environmentally dreadful. The wasteland of the windswept 'open spaces' at the bases of tower blocks; the filth and impersonalization of communal spaces; the useless balconies; and the hearty dislike with which tenants view the robust concrete finishes of their environment give birth to outbreaks of violence against the buildings. The present writer has visited London flats which, only a few weeks after completion had more broken glass in the 'communal' areas than not, while smashed store

[1] *The Failure of 'Housing'*.

doors and unbelievable litter and filth in the 'open spaces', which were useless anyway, completed the depressing picture. The return of families to their homes through a dreadful wasteland of planned and windy dinginess at the bases of tower blocks is one of the most terrible daily events, for the awfulness of such a journey is dismal to contemplate. The colossal failures of our time in this sphere are due to unthinking eclecticism and attitudinizing by politicians, professions and package-deal contractors. The present writer has lived for a period in such a development, and writes from first-hand experience of the unmitigated dreadfulness of it.

The original concepts of tall apartments are found in the ideals of the nineteenth century Utopias, later refined and developed by great minds of the twentieth century, but the originals have little in common with the modern block of council-flats. This debasement of concepts is found in nearly every development in the present century.

Ebenezer Howard's ideas created a small but significant movement which grew to be a modern expression of the solutions which had been at the heart of earlier Utopian schemes. We have mentioned the mandala origins of the garden city in the previous chapter, and although Howard's plans were diagrams, his disciples seem to have overlooked the significance of the mandala forms as symbols of order, of unity and cosmic wholeness. The concept of garden cities give rise to two phenomena both aided and abetted by the motor-car, namely the New Towns and the building of estates of houses in gardens. This latter development was due to several factors. First of all there was a romantic anti-city movement in Victorian times which found early expression in the rush to villadom with the development of railways and tramways. Secondly, there was the arts and crafts movement which helped the trend by encouraging the use of traditional materials and the development of an image of the simple life as a revolt against the ugliness of much of society. It was also associated with socialism which was a strong element in the garden city movement. Thirdly, the development of the internal combustion engine hastened the dispersal of suburbia and made it occur in all directions whereas previously it had been distributed in linear forms associated with trams and railways. Now the city, uncorsetted by fortifications or transport restrictions, could really explode, and as it did so, its diffused areas which mushroomed in the country lost both the benefits of town and country. The middle classes were only of moderate means, and the expression of their desire to live in a house in the country had to be on a small scale, so the watered down ideal became the reality of the dormitory suburb, which was neither town nor country and possessed neither civic nor social consciousness.

After the holocaust of the First World War villadom spread, encouraged by the promises of a 'land fit for heroes'. This is best symbolized at Peacehaven in Sussex. A tremendous increase in housing was achieved in the '20's and '30's, and, especially in Britain and America, this took the form of detached or semi-detached houses on their own plots with gardens. The dream of 'a house in the country' was helped considerably by the large number of speculative builders who developed land in the inter-war period, and the finance was forthcoming from the Building Societies. The political climate of the day had encouraged the image of terrace housing as being synonymous with the term 'slum', and this tendency was helped by the respectability the garden cities had acquired in the meantime. Speculators began developing housing estates and calling them 'garden cities'.

Another factor in the turning away from the tightly constructed urban development was the fear of aerial bombardment which had begun with the Zeppelin raids of the First World War.

Suburbia evolved its own styles, founded on the debasement and misunderstanding of every known form carried to unrecognizable lengths.[1] Its cosiness, its denial of both the scale and essence of town and country, its escapism and its unspeakable smugness have made it a symbol of our society in our time, but its undeniable success financially, both for speculators and purchasers, has assured its survival. Despite the animosity which suburbia creates in sections of society, there is no doubt that the favour with which it is regarded by high finance will aid its perpetuation and renewal. Houses built and sold with profit for a few hundred pounds in the 'thirties are now being disposed of at ten times the original price, or more. This state of affairs is aggravated by the fall in the supply of new dwellings due to planning controls, to the financial climate, and to the shortage of land. The wholesale destruction of residential areas by traffic, businesses and clearance schemes reduces the supply of houses still further.

---

[1] One has seen the great eighteenth century gateposts with their heraldic beasts reduced and debased to two pillars of brickwork, five feet high, capped by two model spaniels picked out in natural colours.

Plate 116: Anarchy. Note the useless grass.

Plate 117: This is supposed to be where people live, but clearly the dominant is now the motor car.

Plate 118: Hilversum Town Hall. Designed by Willem Marinus Dudok.

Plate 119: "Planned Development."

Plate 120: Roehampton.

Plate 121: Roehampton.

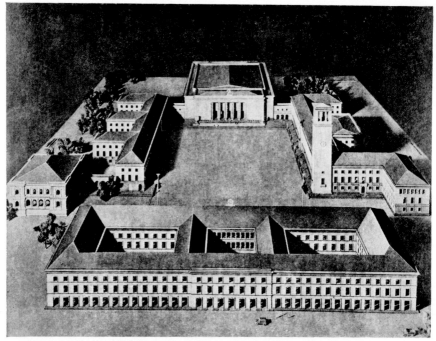

Plate 122: Weimar. Adolf Hitler Platz (Herman Giesler, Architect). (From Neue Deutsche Baukunst.)

Plate 123: Adolf Hitler Platz in Dresden. Wilhelm Kreis, Architect. (From Neue Deutsche Baukunst.)

Plate 124: House of German Art, Munich. Paul Ludwig Troost, Architect. (From Neue Deutsche Baukunst.)

Plate 125: The German Stadium, Nürnberg. Albert Speer, Architect.

Plate 126: Detail from Nürnberg. Albert Speer, Architect. (From Neue Deutsche Baukunst.)

Plate 127: The Lijnbaan, Rotterdam.

Plate 128: The Lijnbaan, Rotterdam.

Plate 129: Eclecticism gone mad. The old Imperial Hotel in Bloomsbury by Fitzroy Doll.

Plate 130: *Enclosure and human scale at Bradford-on-Avon.*

Plate 131: *The terrifying changes in scale. Northampton Square, London, old and new.*

In Britain, as elsewhere in this century, building and planning have been more and more brought within the control of the State. After the Second World War, the new Labour Government brought in legislation for the formation of New Towns in 1946, as well as for planning control, the preparation of development plans by local authorities and for compulsory purchase of land in the Act of 1947. Both Acts were passed in a political climate of idealism and hope after the war, and were deemed essential partly because of urgent need for development due to the cessation of building during the war years, and partly because of war-time destruction.

The New Towns which appeared ringing London after the war owe much to Howard, to the Barlow, Scott and Uthwatt Reports, and to the Greater London Plan of 1944. The Barlow Report came out at a time when the international political climate had deteriorated to the point of war. It recommended that a central national organization should be created to carry out a policy of dispersal by means of satellite towns, and that certain towns should be developed as regional capitals. National planning was in the air, and the war, with the destruction caused by air-raids, helped to create a political climate in which the New Towns would be developed. Inspired by ideals going back to the Utopian socialists, the development of the concept of satellite towns was given physical expression in the post-war years. Small towns of 30,000 to 50,000 people were regarded as being more human than a great metropolis which terrified the idealists. We have noted that Howard did not like gin palaces. One of his disciples wrote that he would have liked to rescue Londoners from London, and that London is a 'great big frightening fact, teeming with life and activity . . .'. He admired London, but, he tells us, he also admired an ant-heap.[1]

Howard advocated a development which could only come about as part of a regional policy. He envisaged a cluster of towns forming a social city focused on the parent city which could provide the facilities which they themselves were too small to support.[2] Many argue that the garden cities would be too small to support the facilities for 'high urban culture',[3] but Howard never intended garden cities to be separate entities, considering them to be part of a pattern on a large mandala form. One of the reasons why a

---

[1] *Early Days in a New Town* p. 121. See Bibliography.
[2] *City and Region* p. 574.
[3] F. J. Osborn's term. See *Big-city Culture: the Reality*.

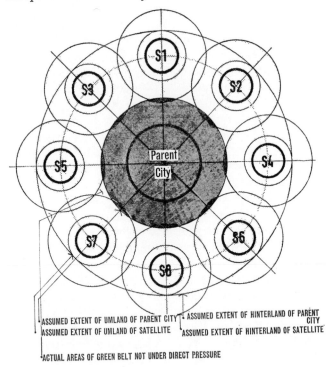

ASSUMED EXTENT OF UMLAND OF PARENT CITY ⌐ ASSUMED EXTENT OF HINTERLAND OF PARENT CITY
ASSUMED EXTENT OF UMLAND OF SATELLITE ⌐ ASSUMED EXTENT OF HINTERLAND OF SATELLITE

⌐ACTUAL AREAS OF GREEN BELT NOT UNDER DIRECT PRESSURE

Diagram: satellite towns   Figure No. 31

large population is needed to support such facilities is the fact that 'high urban culture' is only popular among very few people. This is partly due to the type of thinking which has developed from the Renaissance onwards that 'culture' is something for the upper classes and therefore is separated out from the rest of society.

The New Towns policy, nevertheless, was developed with scant regard for regional implications. The Green Belts, which were supposed to be reserved for agriculture, woods, and recreation, have come under intolerable pressure with almost universal car owner-ship. Not only does a metropolis have its umland and hinterland, but so does each satellite town, so areas on the outer fringes of the metropolis come under two sets of pressures: those of the metropolis itself, and those of its satellites. As cities tend to be almost fully built up, any 'slum clearance' causes 'overspill' population which has to be re-housed in a satellite, since redevelopment of a 'slum' district will usually put fewer people back on the site. Shortage of land for building has inflated the prices of land and property, and created a situation where districts, formerly utterly run-down, are being bought up and rehabilitated at fantastic prices by people desperate for accommodation. Many local authorities, imbued with the zeal of righteous hatred of anything older than the present century, have been busy laying waste many areas which could have been rehabilitated, but since such areas have probably been under 'redevelopment' threat for some time, private enterprise obviously has not invested to make good the property. As a result of all these factors, Green Belts tend to be over-used, with far too high a density of 'recreational use'. The spectacle of the weekend motorist and his family enjoying the 'amenity' of a lay-by is a common one and symbolizes the half-baked use of leisure in areas under tremendous pressure from both the metropolis and its satellites.

The New Towns were not laid out with formal considerations, but were divided into 'neighbourhood units' linked to the town centre. Open spaces are much in evidence, and industry is separately zoned. This century has had a fondness for lots of grass, and housing estates and New Towns have any amount of it: much is useless, in the form of grass strips at the sides of roads, or as semibald patches which add an undeveloped air of scruffiness to the townscape. Concepts such as the breaking down of the towns into units separated by landscape has tended to create isolated 'estates' merely linked to the centre by paths and roads. There is thus little sense of visual cohesion or unity, despite the success in other ways of the New Towns, and inscape, let us face it, is absent. The new dominants, despite the ideals, are the roads and the centres composed of the branches of the same nation-wide commercial enterprises. The identical supermarkets, chain stores, banks, building societies and public offices predominate: the ruling elements are now the big businesses, and it does not matter if the monopolies are 'public' or 'private'. The same uniformity, the same commercial brashness and the same deadly dullness dominate the centres of the New Towns.

The philistinism and the essential destructiveness of the new dominants may be seen in London. The wonderful skyline which Wren created has disappeared as the offices of innumerable corporations have risen to dominate the City. St. Paul's alone still stands out, and only because it is so big. The offices, the growth of bureaucracy and of the snobbery of white-collarism as opposed to creative work betray a political climate of spiritual exhaustion: of an age which specializes in insignificance, in the fond belief that their addition and collation will add up to something of importance. Cars are everywhere, fouling the air and filling the streets with the filth of their exhausts, while roads for cars cut through the urban matrix, making nonsense of the existing structure and creating a new and gross scale which is related to turning-circles and not to people. Roads beget traffic, yet more roads appear, for we are told that the car is necessary to the economy.

It is clear that the new dominants of office-blocks, roads, commerce and bureaucracy are expressive of a new dictatorship, whether in government or business. Aided by the institutions and the system of meritocracy, the new dictatorships can order the environment while remaining anonymous. The results of their efforts drive the human spirit to despair in the face of such monstrous inhumanity, for the new powers are unaware of the possibilities and nature of art,[1] looking on it as something unnecessary and suspect. Obviously they abhor everything which is not either a parody of, a watered down expression of, or a reaction against a genuine expression of creation. The only art which is valuable to such elements is that which is an investment. A Gothic cathedral is an expression of art: a municipal coat-of-arms applied to the façade of a new town hall is not.

Order in urban design has been in retreat, and one of the reasons for this is the growth of specialization, leading to a lack of understanding of the wholeness of life. The Biosphere itself has been chopped up and compartmented, controlled by various 'experts', while the Noösphere has been generally ignored. Specialization has meant the losing of the mandala conception of cosmic wholeness in the obscurities and futilities of a mass of detail. Institutionalism has tended to encourage specialization on the grounds that universal men are either impossible or out of date. A new totality of vision is necessary to restore unity, for the eclecticism, chaos, lack of direction and sheer ugliness of the contemporary situation demand an all-embracing creative approach. Further specialization and more rules and regulations cannot create a cohesion.

---

[1] 'Art', in such a society becomes something which is applied, as a concession, to a building or a town. It usually takes the form of a coat-of-arms or a piece of 'decorative sculpture', and as such is entirely meaningless as art.

OTHER DEVELOPMENTS

It is significant that H. P. Berlage, the great architect who did so much fine work in Amsterdam, should have rejected the garden city concept. Amsterdam had a long tradition of architecture and planning, and the developments in this century added an extension to the existing town linked to and integrated with the old city. Satellites were thus rejected. Berlage proposed the first plan in 1902, and revision followed in 1915. The Housing Act of 1901 required each town in Holland of over 10,000 people to produce detailed and general plans for their future development. Berlage was asked to produce the development plan for Amsterdam, and in his work he created unified streetscapes with sensitively planted pavements, as a re-interpretation of nineteenth century precedents. After 1934, Amsterdam was planned by a public department, and a policy of the breaking up of physical units by landscaping as a departure from nineteenth century practice was pursued, as a forerunner of new towns elsewhere. Aesthetic control was retained by the municipality, a very ancient control which goes back to mediaeval times. In Amsterdam South, the dominants became the housing which was largely erected by co-operative housing groups. Holland wisely avoided involvement in the First World War, and a long tradition of making the best possible use of land and an equally long tradition of approaching city building with sensitivity and care for the corporate good of the citizens helped to create towns and extensions which feel as though they have grown organically. Breaks between country and town are clean in Holland, and something of the mediaeval self-contained character is maintained there. The half-world of much of the open space round cities in Britain is avoided, for every square inch of land in Holland is positively used.

In the Netherlands, where urban tradition is very strong, one of the finest expressions of the garden city type of development is at Hilversum, which embodies many of Howard's ideas. Hilversum is spacious and charming, with nature playing a positive part, and not reduced to bald grass verges and a few cherry trees. The town is an 'infill' in the settlement structure of the Netherlands, and, in a sense, is a satellite of Amsterdam, although it, like Howard's garden city, is a community in itself. Hilversum owes much to the quality of the work of Dudok, whose Stadhuis is a noble expression of twentieth century architecture integrated with nature.

The Zeitgeist of the nineteenth century lived on to the First

World War. The destruction of men, materials and ideals changed the political climate entirely, and destroyed European hegemony. The break up of the empires and the revolutions which gave birth to so many smaller states ruled by socialistic governments heralded the true twentieth century.

In the U.S.S.R., of course, a completely socialist state was founded, and ideas which had stemmed from the west were given expression in the Union. A political climate created in the destruction of the Romanov empire was favourable to the putting into practice of theories which had developed from the writings of the middle-class Karl Marx and Friedrich Engels. Russia was for a brief while the Mecca of intellectuals. Constructivism, Miliutin's linear designs for Magnetogorsk, socialism and experiments in the arts, however, soon lost their impetus in a political climate of totalitarian repression which expressed itself in the heavy and de-based classicism of the Stalin era.

In the west, new ideals, especially in Germany, gave birth to the founding of the Bauhaus in 1919 as an attempt to re-unite architecture and contemporary activities, especially in the industrial field. Walter Gropius, the founder, surrounded himself with talented men from many spheres: Klee, Schlemmer, Kandinsky, Moholy-Nagy and Breuer, among others, and, after the school moved to Dessau, it became even more involved in industry and produced answers to design problems of the day. The basic tenet of the Bauhaus philosophy was to direct creative efforts into a unity having a basis in humanity, harnessing mechanization and not reacting against it.

Gropius had been intimately associated with the Deutsche Werkbund, the aim of which was to achieve better workmanship and better quality in mass-produced goods, giving young talent a chance to prove its worth. Workers, industrialists and artists were to contribute to this ideal. The Deutsche Werkbund had concepts which could be traced back to the English industrial reformers. Perhaps its finest achievement was the Cologne exhibition in the fateful year of 1914, but the war did not kill the idealism of the Werkbund. In the political climate of the 'twenties, when social democracy had replaced the nineteenth century pageantry and neo-baroque magnificence of the Wilhelmian Empire, the avant-garde was given freedom of expression officially. Ludwig Mies van der Rohe became Vice President of the Werkbund, and he encouraged the development of Dutch ideas on housing, arranging for an international group of architects to contribute to the Weissenhof housing scheme

Saynätsalo community centre

Weissenhof settlement, Stuttgart

Aalto and Mies van der Rohe   Figure No. 32

at Stuttgart. J. J. P. Oud, who had done much work in Holland, and Le Corbusier both built for this project. The importance of the Weissenhof experiment was that it embodied all the new ideas of rational planning and modern construction. Villadom, however, took immediately recognizable motifs, such as the balcony railings of Mies van der Rohe's scheme, and applied them to the suburban semi-detached, so that a new variant was obtained, namely the 'modernistic' house. Again, eclecticism and unthinking use of small visual details had made a mockery of the original idea. In later years, Mies van der Rohe's apartment blocks in Chicago have had a tremendous effect on tall blocks of offices and flats, debased and made crude in the interpretation, it is true, and as such, eclecticism is again rampant.

Le Corbusier's work in town design which developed in the 'twenties and 'thirties has become a potent example. His use of the

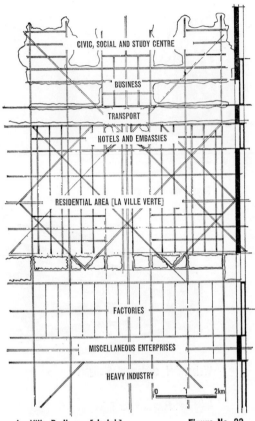

CIVIC, SOCIAL AND STUDY CENTRE

BUSINESS

TRANSPORT

HOTELS AND EMBASSIES

RESIDENTIAL AREA [LA VILLE VERTE]

FACTORIES

MISCELLANEOUS ENTERPRISES

HEAVY INDUSTRY

0   1   2km

La Ville Radieuse [sketch]   Figure No. 33

dominant motifs of skyscrapers set amid greenery achieved its ulti-
mate expression in *La Ville Radieuse* of 1933. Both *La Ville Contem-
poraine* of 1922 and *La Ville Radieuse* pay great attention to transport
problems and to the zoning of activities, and both plans are notable
for their axes, symmetry and mandala remnants. *La Ville Contem-
poraine* even had triumphal arches.

Le Corbusier also designed linear towns for Algiers and Zlin, the
last for the Bata corporation. It is curious how spatial relationships
of the late baroque age and those of neo-classicism are very near
some of Le Corbusier's planning work.

In individual buildings Le Corbusier's constructional techniques
and surface treatments have had a profound effect, because his work
has entered into the vocabulary of designers. His social imagination[1]

---

[1] Giedion's term. See *Space, Time and Architecture* p. 531.

gave rise to the *Unité d'Habitation* which was an attempt to re-unify individuals with the group. But, and here is a big *but*, the concepts which, handled by the master might have worked, have now been imitated and parodied without an understanding of the inner nature of what Le Corbusier was trying to do. Apartment blocks and offices rise in housing estates and town centres, not sur-rounded by open park, but with a few square feet of useless open space at the bases. Tall blocks of flats and offices create windy con-ditions at the bottom, making any 'open space' highly unpleasant to use. Socially, the debased 'apartment block' creates great prob-lems of loneliness and isolation as well as the practical difficulties of supervising children at play. The trouble is that individual build-ings by masters of the modern movement have been taken out of context, misinterpreted and parodied, so that the environment created has no sense and no meaning.[1]

Le Corbusier's work must be seen as a development within a tradition and not as an isolated phenomenon. Otto Wagner and the Vienna school, which had in turn been influenced by Mackin-tosh, played an important part in the dissemination of ideas, so that by the time Sant 'Elia came to design his *Città Nuova*, various con-cepts such as multi-level service routes, tall apartment blocks and sophisticated vertical circulation were incorporated in it. Sant 'Elia and the Futurists undoubtedly contributed significantly to the de-velopment of ideas to which Le Corbusier later gave new expression and new life, and the most notable of these concepts was that of a dynamic view of space.

In mediaeval times, spaces were inter-related and buildings were framed by streets and other buildings.[2] The town, however, was an object in space, walled and complete. Le Corbusier and his pre-decessors developed the concept of placing large buildings in space, either related formally, as in his *La Ville Radieuse*, or informally, as at St. Dié and Zlin.

The *Unités d'Habitation* owe much to nineteenth century Uto-pian ideas such as the *Phalanstère*, for their interior streets, nurseries, gymnasia and theatre, and the *Unités*, of which the best, in the

---

[1] A few holes punched in a concrete wall in a regular fashion were described to me by the architect in charge of the job as 'being influenced by Ronchamp.' That a profound and significant building such as Ronchamp should be so fundamentally misunderstood as to be compared with a screen wall in a muni-cipal car park by a professional architect is a source of sober reflection.

[2] See Camillo Sitte's studies.

present writer's opinion, is the Marseilles block, are essentially objects in space.

Many slab blocks throughout western Europe owe much in *appearance* to Le Corbusier's projects, but they are not themselves products of the social imagination which gave the *raison d'être* to the *Unités*. The *Unité d'Habitation* was an attempt to take a number of housing units and to combine them within one construction with other human needs. Slab blocks of flats, purely residential, and with an exterior resemblance to the *Unités* because of the use of 'pilotis', balconies, lift towers and concrete finishes, are expressions of a new eclecticism.

Alvar Aalto of Finland has produced much work of great beauty in which he has attempted to unify the organic and inorganic. His project for Ouln (1943) had much of the gentleness and strength of previous centuries, while his Saynätsalo is a wonderful union of nature and buildings. The spiritual element in Aalto's work seems to the present writer to be very strong, and perhaps only he in this century has consistently been aware of the need to cater for the Noösphere in human activities. At the same time it must be remembered that Finland is a country with a small population constantly in touch with nature. This northern land is particularly responsive to such things as seasonal changes, and spring has a real meaning, much more so that in the urbanized societies of Europe and America. The use of natural materials in building is a feature of Finnish architecture, and this emphasizes the contact with nature.

Linear concepts in town design were embodied in the MARS Plan for London of 1937–1939 prepared under the chairmanship of Arthur Korn. This plan was notable for its unity, in that the problems of London were considered as a part of a whole and living organism, and attempts were made to co-ordinate the factors of housing, work and amenities, linking them by means of essentially linear systems of transport. The various centres which were incorporated in the scheme were to have architectural identity and so form dominants 'so essential for the visual articulation of a vast urban area.' The scale of thinking in the MARS Plan was large, and 'district units' were proposed of 500,000 people each. The politico-cultural nature of society was to be expressed in the buildings of social and community life, and the enhancing of the aesthetic value of the town were among the objectives of the scheme.[1]

[1] *History Builds the Town* pp. 89 and 90.

Unité d'Habitation at Briey-en-Forêt
(from a drawing by the author)

Figure No. 33a

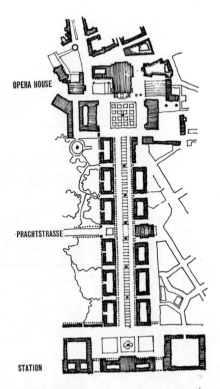

PROJECT FOR THE 'HITLERZENTRUM': NAZI CULTURAL CAPITAL AT LINZ

Nazi town design   Figure No. 34

The political climate established in Germany in 1933 drove the entire avant-garde out of the country. A Germanic national spirit expressed in cities goes back to some examples of early mediaeval times, but the modern concept of a city as an expression of ideals of pan-Germanism begins with Fichte, who drew attention to the tremendous achievements of free cities in artistic fields. Later, Sitte extolled the mediaeval new towns, and the Nazi planners seem to have agreed with Sitte in his admiration for them.

Nazi totalitarianism expressed itself in debased neo-classicism and in neo-baroque vistas. Hitler's project for the European cultural capital at Linz shows a renewal of classical formalism, while Mussolini's unfinished shell of New Rome remains a grandiose and overpowering symbol of his aspirations to neo-imperial grandeur.

Linz, the provincial Austrian city, where Hitler attended school, was to be the Nazi capital to house the looted art from all over the conquered world. A 'Hitlerzentrum' was to be composed of an axial street with an opera house at one end and a railway station at the other. Cultural buildings housing various galleries were to line the main street, the Prachtstrasse.[1]

Wilhelm Kreis produced a neo-classical design for the Adolf-Hitler Platz in Dresden which owes something to Schinkel. The same architect designed a monumental *Soldatenhalle* for Berlin which had enormous twin simplified classical columns and heroic but coarse sculpture. This was to be part of a complex of the *Oberkommandos des Heeres* near the Tiergarten. Hermann Giesler's Adolf-Hitler Platz in Weimar is smaller in scale than Kreis's Dresden scheme, but has neo-classical similarity. Paul Ludwig Troost carried out much work in München, and his *Haus der Deutschen Kunst* is a good example of his style, which incorporated a monumental and simplified classicism in serried rows of columns. This building is extremely coarsely detailed, and the planning is archaic.

The monumental façadism of the architecture of the Third Reich was an essential backcloth to the parades and public spectacle so characteristic of totalitarian régimes. The need for display and monumentality has already been noted in earlier civilizations, and it appeared again in Nazi Germany. Like the Romans under the Empire, the Nazis erected enormous buildings where thousands o people could gather at any one time.

The name of Albert Speer crops up in connection with the tower of the German pavilion in the Paris exhibition of 1937 which he designed. There was a startling similarity in spirit between this and the U.S.S.R. pavilion, except that Speer's work was more refined. The 1937 pavilion is an amazing reaction compared with the German pavilion at Barcelona only eight years previously.

Speer designed the great parade-ground complex for the party capital of Nürnberg. His monumental axially planned schemes are on a colossal scale, and the Zeppelinfeld and Deutsche Stadion were exercises in hugeness which easily surpass Parisian examples and come nearer imperial Rome in spirit.[2]

The reactionary nature of the Nazi political climate is symbolized in its backward looking architectural expressions and in its debased

[1] See *The Jackdaw of Linz*.
[2] A collection of Nazi buildings in photographs was published in 1941 under the title *Neue Deutsche Baukunst*.

neo-classical art. Speer's work did rise above the general level of Nazi architecture, and his grandiose schemes are well-detailed, but, taken as a whole, there is a deadness and a stifling reactionary feeling about Nazi design.

Soviet Russian and East German efforts in Berlin have demonstrated visibly the soulless pomposity of totalitarian government. In the Stalin Allee the mindless and bastardized design, sadly reminiscent of much commercial and municipal development in Britain, betrays the real nature of the forces behind such schemes: unfeeling and philistine reactionaries under whose rule creative art cannot express itself.

Austria was one of the places where large-scale housing developed earliest. The Werkbundsiedlung of 1932 and the Karl Marx Hof of 1930 are well known. The latter, a socialist housing settlement of tremendously strong construction was actually used as a fortress by the workers during the civil war of the 'thirties when workers and government troops fought in the streets of Vienna.

In Holland, the political climate has long been democratic in nature, and the sensitivity and scale of urban development in the Netherlands have been examples to the world. Since the war, the Lijnbaan shopping centre in bombed Rotterdam has been completed: a two-storied pedestrian precinct with nearby apartment development, concert hall, railway station and commercial centre. It is a good example of modern planning, with emphasis on human activity. It can safely be said that the dominating spirit in the Lijnbaan, Rotterdam, is its humanity. Yet even here the architecture is unsuccessful. The crudity of the expression and the sheer ugliness of the Lijnbaan and the whole area are sad indictments of any age where expediency has replaced imagination and the cosmic beat no longer enters into the design of cities.

CONCLUSION

The design of towns expresses much of the social and political mood of a civilization as well as primarily the nature of the dominant sectors in a society. In a true democracy the scope of creative patronage is very wide, while in a totalitarian state it is extremely narrow. Ideally, the design of towns should reflect the nature, aspirations and degree of sophistication acquired by their inhabitants, but in most civilizations only the dominant ruling classes order the Zeitgeist and therefore only favoured art forms can flourish.

Ambrose Bierce said that public opinion is the negligible factor in government. Our brief study has attempted to show how the ruling elements have determined the environment, and the political climate is determined by these elements, which permit or order a physical expression of their inner nature in the design of towns. Public opinion, only if mobilized by leadership and moulded by it, can have any effect on political climate. This is a Marxist view, and is a central call to the forcible overthrow of existing social orders. Such revolutions are urban ones.

Urban man expresses himself and his aspirations in the design of cities. Cities have determined history, and the city symbolizes the rule of elements totally the antithesis of the countryside. Cities which have been creative are very different from non-creative ones, and thus we have two types of city: culture-cities, and civilization cities.[1] Civilization, to Spengler, was the dead phase of a culture, whereas culture, to him, meant the creative, living part of an historic development. The modern city consists of unresolved tensions, and the relaxations of the civilization-city are only distractions of the most trite kind, while genuine play, in the Dionysian sense of inebriation, ecstasy and periodical abandonment to the senses, are seen as part of a 'cosmic beat' no longer comprehensible to a civilized society.

Today, the cosmic view is missing: we are all specialists. Societies, or their ruling elements, do not possess the universal vision, appreciating as it were, Apollo and Dionysus simultaneously. Losing the meaning of a totality because of attention to detail is a fundamental disease of our age, yet the re-unification of all facets of life is possible in cities designed with that in view, although this is only possible with a change of heart in the dominant members of society or their replacement.

Cities are in danger from the machines man has created, and recent thoughts on traffic in towns face up to this problem: but it is not just cars, the crumbling fabric of our older cities, and changing social habits that are causes for concern. It is the curious sterility and continued compartmenting of civilization that are sinister, where even death is made insignificant and has lost not its terror but its reality. The distressing gentility of the disposal of corpses without ceremony in the municipal incinerator suburbanizes even death. In culture-societies, death is significant, and is celebrated with uninhibited ceremony as a symbol of the end of a cycle. The hurried

[1] Spengler's terms.

suburban modern funeral is symbolic of our civilization's distaste for the realities of human existence and is very different from the ceremonial of cultured societies. The American funeral is a denial of reality in another way, made possible by a more affluent society.

A culture-city is infinitely richer than the anthill, for it conveys significance and spirituality to an existence which otherwise would be rooted in the Biosphere alone, amputated from the Noösphere. Between ideal cities and cities conceived empirically using data applicable to the Biosphere there is a gap: by bringing them together negatively, they must inevitably clash; but if, in a political climate where Snow's 'two cultures' could once more be united, the cohesion could be positive, in that Biosphere and Noösphere could join in mandala unity.

The history of politics and aesthetics is a history of dominants: the dominant ideas of a dominant group help us to see into a culture or a civilization, and the study of its dominants in cities helps us to gain an insight into the nature of a society. In all history, the models of reality express and create the reality. A Gothic cathedral, a baroque vista, a ziggurat, a pyramid or a skyscraper are not only the result of a Zeitgeist: they are responsible for its realization. The world readily responds to models, and it is in the political climate created by the dominants of a society that the models are made to mould society.

Towns are designed and constructed in relation to a Zeitgeist in which an ideology has gained acceptance and usually been adulterated. A revolution of ideas creates a social order through the leading elements of that society accepting and adapting the ideas or being overthrown by other leading elements. Either way, the interpretation of the ideology is more important than the original, for the interpretation of reality creates it.[1]

Goethe was concerned with the disenchantment of his own age, and, significantly, it was in his time that the estrangement between symbols and reality was finally made absolute after the furious and passionate attempt of the baroque to re-unite them. In Goethe's scientific discourses we get a clue as to the nature and enormity of the problem, when he warns us that history has to be re-written every now and then not because of new discoveries but because our point of vision has changed.

---

[1] Compare the original expressions of the modern movement with the average development of today.

The design of human environment today is beset by theories, dogma, political attitudinizing and specialization. Theories have been accepted as reality, and fashions have replaced ideas in an eclecticism of gross absurdity ten thousand times more ridiculous than Victorian eclecticism, which at least was amusing and well executed. Goethe warned us of the dangers of setting up theories in fiction and science because of such theories being set up as images, worshipped, and then regarded as truth and reality.

Burckhardt has been mentioned often in this study, and his *Reflections on History* and the *Civilization of the Renaissance in Italy* have both served to illuminate facets of the history of culture. What comes out in Burckhardt's writings is his sadness at the declining sense of significance in his own age. Spiritual exhaustion has been the concern of many writers of the present century, such as Kafka and D. H. Lawrence. The prosaicness of the Zeitgeist made many intellectuals turn to socialism, but Oswald Spengler warned prior to 1917 that 'Hard as the half-developed Socialism of today is fighting against expansion, one day it will become arch-expansionist itself. . .'.[1] 'We have to reckon with the hard cold facts of a *late* life, to which the parallel is to be found . . . in Caesar's Rome.'[2] Spengler also draws our attention to the declining importance of philosophy in his lifetime.[3] He anticipates Snow's 'two cultures', but sees dangers that Snow does not seem to acknowledge. A political climate in any society, as we have seen, is the result of dominant models, and these are symbolized in dominant elements in town design. If a society is spiritually exhausted, two things can happen: it can express its exhaustion for a while in eclecticism, for Spengler asserts that truly creative possibilities had long been exhausted by his day; or it can expand, just as Roman Caesarism encouraged the expansion of the Empire. A totalitarian state, whether subject to a *politburo* or an emperor-dictator, indulges in wars of aggression, has a slave labour system, and builds monuments to itself in pompous and reactionary styles. The spiritual nature of a society ruled by Caesars, whether they be party Caesars or monopolist Caesars, will not be fertile, and 'culture' will be singled out from society as a thing apart, screened to make sure it is acceptable to the régime.

Classical man, Spengler insists, willed to have no history, for in the days of Aristotle, it was not really known if Leucippus had ever

[1] *The Decline of the West* Vol. I, p. 37.
[2] *Ibid.* p. 40.
[3] *Ibid.* p. 42.

existed.[1] Myth and history merged, even for contemporaries of the event, whereas, in 'civilized' societies, decadent by Spengler's standards, all the works of dead cultures are collected in museums, deprived of that moment of purpose which gave them their existence. In western civilization, the collection of memorials and relics of the past dates from Renaissance times, as Burckhardt tells us. The cultural ghetto, separated out from the body of the city, is one of the disasters of contemporary life. Howard separated it out in his diagram for the 'garden city', and London's South Bank is a symptom of the same disease. What possible *meaning* can a complex of theatres, concert halls and possibly an opera house on a windswept bank of concrete symbolize? Obviously the complete sundering of 'culture' in inverted commas from the rest of society. 'Culture' is now selected, grilled and dissected by the arbiters of taste, placed in a museum, subsidized and paid for by the State, and exhibited in its ghetto as a diversion for a society no longer daily and actively engaged in acts of creation, but encouraged by specialized mass-education and Pavlovian conditioning to attitudinizing instead of honest criticism.

'High urban culture'[2] is something which only a small minority enjoys, and it is determined by the ruling caste through the arbiters and selectors. Its physical separation in an 'arts centre' apart from the rest of a city merely emphasizes its 'civilization' aspect as opposed to its 'cultural' one, as well as its lack of relevance to society in general. Sir Frederic Osborn has calculated that the average Parisian goes to the Louvre once every 28 years.[3]

Dominants in urban cultures are linked with dominant groups. Power and finance determine the monuments of the Zeitgeist, and the holders of the power and the controllers of the finance determine the function, the form and the quality of the monuments. Institutions have allied with the powerful dominants, and have an interest in obtaining the patronage of the holders of power. Today, more than ever before, the established specialists who are patronized by the power groups create the environments in which we live. That these specialists have done enormous harm to our cities and towns is self-evident. They have betrayed the trust given them, and they have sold their integrity for material gain. Specialization

[1]   *The Decline of the West* Vol. I, p. 135.
[2]   F. J. Osborn's term.
[3]   *New Towns Come of Age* p. 46.

is partly responsible for the confounding of ideas in our day and the decline in the arts coincides with grave problems such as those of the city, land-depopulation, the position of the individual in relation to the state, pollution, and the crises of socialism and materialism.

The dominant monuments of our time, such as the skyscrapers of the great monopolies, demonstrate the impact upon the visual face of a town by dominants of a society. The separation of Biosphere and Noösphere has created a lack of unity in our civilization and contributed to the loss of feeling in so much of our environment. Specialized disciplines have made islands of aspects of education, so that they look at each other, as it were, with mutual suspicion and fear. There is a lacking of sensibility, a loss of scale, an absence of humanity in nearly every major modern development in the twentieth century, with only a few exceptions. Techniques have advanced, systems have developed, but feeling has been swept under the carpet. The two cultures have created a schizophrenic society which glibly discusses scientific method, systems and technology without any thought as to where it is all leading. Methodology and systems for their own sake can be the tools of untold horrors, unless a philosophy based on the re-integration of the separated facets of life guides them.

Dramatic and catastrophic events in history, we believe, were caused by personalities of colossal size which strode across the stage of the world and changed its nature. But what if society, as heir to this notion which had come down from history, attempted to avoid catastrophe by turning to mediocrity, in the hope, vain as it turns out, that a safe and cosy civilization would result? Such a view, with its dislike of the 'prima donna' in architecture and planning and its belief in committees, teams and data banks would account for much. It is, however, a falsehood to believe that colossi are responsible for the disasters of the past, for such a concept does not take into consideration the daemonic nature of mediocrity.

Mediocrity has a destructive power, for in a world disenchanted with myth and poetry, concerned only with attitudinizing and the mean, the hero-less city will be peopled by savages living in all mod. con. apartments, earning their living by serving machines, monopolies and 'society'; pulling levers and pressing buttons in a mindless series of specialized compartments. It is as though in a nightmare world of non-comprehension, emptiness and the negation of worth had replaced nobility, sensibility and intellect. In another culture the disasters of contemporary environment would have been seen in their true light, as the work of hostile elements which exist off the carrion of received ideas and faithfully attitudinize instead of create.

An improved technology has not been matched by the continuing potency of creative imagination. It was Karl Kraus who showed us the dreadful possibilities of mediocrity in his *Last Days of Mankind*. Mediocrity shrinks from exposing itself to the influence of greatness and to the reality which can only be understood through the symbol. Modern minds have surrendered to a world ruled by the statistician, where all experience is reduced to a data bank from which the Noösphere must necessarily be excluded. Pedantry is no substitute for creative imagination.

Since so much of our urban structure is being torn apart and so much of new development has little sense of order or humanity as expedient solutions are found to problems which are fundamental in our society, we must find a remedy before we have destroyed all we possess. The political climate today is one of utter confusion, as our systems, our institutions and our economic base show grave disturbances. Our urban chaos reflects social dissolution.

There are signs of change, however. The young are questioning everything, but have turned to new pop-gods and to the mythology of tin-pan alley culture in an attempt, one suspects, to find the missing Noösphere in life. Revolt is in the air, and there are indications that the widespread disillusionment with the *status quo* could give rise to a collective will to inner change, but it could also result in collapse of all order, urban or otherwise. The turning to unreason and illusion is a source of disquiet, for is seems untempered by any balancing factor at present.

Symbolically, a union of Dionysus and Apollo, recognizing that life is diversification, could create the joyous acceptance of the wholeness of things. The god of ecstasy and unreason and the god of order and light, separated by convention and pseudo-moralistic legislation, could, by their very contradiction, create a whole. Biosphere and Noösphere could unite, reconciled by contradiction, and held together in a symbol: the mandala form of the living culture-city.

General Bibliography

ARISTOTLE

The North British Mail, June 20
Glasgow, 1849
Politics
Tr. John Warrington
London and New York, 1959

BENEVOLO, LEONARDO

The Origins of Modern Town Planning
Tr. Judith Lantry
London, 1967

BERESFORD, MAURICE

New Towns of the Middle Ages: Town plantation
in England, Wales and Gascony
London, 1967

BIBLE, THE HOLY

King James version

BONNARD, ANDRÉ

Greek Civilization
London, 1958

BOWRA, C. M.

The Greek Experience
London, 1957

BREASTED, J. H.

Ancient Times
London, 1914

BUCKINGHAM, JAMES S.

*National Evils and Practical Remedies, with the Plan
of a Model Town*
London, 1849

BURCKHARDT, JACOB

The Age of Constantine the Great
Tr. Moses Hadas
London, 1949
Reflections on History
Tr. M.D.H.
London, 1947
The Civilization of the Renaissance in Italy
Tr. S. G. C. Middlemore
Vienna and London, 1937

CAMBLIN, GILBERT

The Town in Ulster
Belfast, 1951

CARVER, HUMPHREY

Cities in the Suburbs
Toronto, 1962

CLARK, KENNETH — *The Nude*
Harmondsworth, 1960
The Gothic Revival
London, 1928

COLLINS, GEORGE R., and
COLLINS, CHRISTIANE C. — *Camillo Sitte and the Birth of Modern City Planning*
London, 1965

COULTON, GEORGE GORDON — *Life in the Middle Ages*
Cambridge, 1930

CURL, JAMES STEVENS — Article in the *R.I.B.A. Journal* of April, 1968

DALTON, O. M. — *Byzantine Art and Archaeology*
New York, 1961

DANTE ALIGHIERI — *The Divine Comedy*
Various editions

DICKINSON, R. E. — *The West European City*
London, 1951
City and Region
London, 1964

DISRAELI, BENJAMIN — *Sybil, or The Two Nations*
London, 1845
The City Region in Western Europe
London, 1967 (a revised version of City and Region)
The German Lebensraum
Harmondsworth, 1943

DODDS, GORDON — See WILKES, LYALL

DOUGLAS, NORMAN — *Old Calabria*
Harmondsworth, 1962

ENGELS, F. — *The Condition of the Working Classes in England in 1844*
Tr. Wischnewetzky
London, 1892

ETTLINGER, L. G. — Article 'The Duke of Wellington's Funeral Car' in the *Journal of the Warburg and Courtauld Institutes*, III, 1939
Article 'On Science, Industry and Art. Some Theories of Gottfried Semper' in the *Architectural Review*, Vol. CXXXVI, July, 1964

EVELYN, JOHN — *The Diary*
London, 1879

FLETCHER, SIR BANISTER   *A History of Architecture on the Comparative Method*
London. Various editions

FRANKFORT, H.   *The Art and Architecture of the Ancient Orient*
Harmondsworth, 1954

GARDNER, H.   *The Metaphysical Poets*
(Editor)   Harmondsworth, 1957

GEDDES, PATRICK, and   *Life: Outlines of Biology*
THOMSON, J. ARTHUR   New York, 1931

GIEDION, S.   *The Eternal Present*, Vols. I and II
New York, 1962 and 1964
Space, Time and Architecture
Cambridge, Mass. and London, 1962

GIBBON, EDWARD   *The Decline and Fall of the Roman Empire*
Various editions

GIBBON, MONK   *Western Germany*
London, 1955

GOETHE, JOHANN   *Wilhelm Meister* and other works
WOLFGANG VON   Various editions

GREEN, F. H. W.   Article in *Geography*, Vol. 34, p. 89, 1949

GUTKIND, E. A.   *International History of City Development*
Vol. I, Urban Development in Central Europe
New York, 1964

HAMILTON, J. ARNOTT   *Byzantine Architecture and Decoration*
London, 1933

HEAP, DESMOND   *An Outline of Planning Law*
London, 1963

HEARSEY, JOHN E. N.   *City of Constantine* 324–1453
London, 1963

HEGEMANN, WERNER, and   *The American Vitruvius: An Architects'*
PEETS, ELBERT   *Handbook of Civic Art*
New York, 1922

HELLER, ERICH   *The Disinherited Mind*
Harmondsworth, 1961

HOLROYD, ABRAHAM   *Saltaire and its Founder*
Saltaire, 1871

HOWARD, EBENEZER   *Garden Cities of Tomorrow*
London, 1945

HUGHES, T. H., and   *Towns and Town Planning*
LAMBORN, E. A. G.   Oxford, 1923

JUNG, C. G., and
VON FRANZ, M-L
(Editors)

Man and his Symbols
London, 1964

KAFKA, FRANZ

The Castle
Tr. W. & E. Muir and E. Wilkins and
E. Kaiser
Harmondsworth, 1957

KÄHLER, HEINZ

Rome and her Empire
Tr. J. R. Foster
Baden-Baden and London, 1963

KNIGHT, CHARLES
(Editor)

London, Vol. IV
Corrected by E. Walford
London, 1841–44

KORN, ARTHUR

History Builds the Town
London, 1953

KRIESIS, PAUL

Article 'Metropolitan Centres' in
The Architects' Year Book No. 9
London, 1960

LAMBERT, S. (*et al.*)

Article 'New Lanark' in *The Architects' Journal*
of 16th May, 1964

LAMBORN, E. A. G.

See HUGHES, T. H.

LLOYD, JOHN H.

*The History, Topography and Antiquities of
Highgate in the County of Middlesex*
Highgate, 1888

LYNCH, KEVIN

The Image of the City
Cambridge, Mass. 1960

MARX, KARL

Capital
London, 1938
Manifesto of the Communist Party
Moscow, 1935
Selected Works
London, 1945

MAYHEW, HENRY

London's Underworld
(Edited by P. Quennell)
London, 1950

MIDDLEBROOK, S.

Newcastle-upon-Tyne. Its Growth and Achievement
Newcastle, 1950

MOGEY, J.

Rural Life in Northern Ireland
London, 1947

MUMFORD, LEWIS

The Culture of Cities
London, 1938

MUMFORD, LEWIS—cont.   *The Condition of Man*
                        London, 1944

NIETZSCHE, FRIEDRICH W. *Complete Works*
                        New York, 1927

OSBORN, F. J.   Article 'Early Days in a New Town' in
                        New Towns Come of Age, a special issue of
                        Town and Country Planning
                        January–February, 1968
                        Article 'Big-city Culture: the Reality' in
                        New Towns Come of Age, a special issue of
                        Town and Country Planning for
                        January–February, 1968

OWEN, ROBERT   *A New View of Society*
                        London, 1818

PEETS, ELBERT   See HEGEMANN, WERNER

PEROWNE, STEWART   *The End of the Roman World*
                        London, 1966

PEVSNER, NIKOLAUS   *An Outline of European Architecture*
                        Harmondsworth, 1964
                        Pioneers of Modern Design
                        Harmondsworth, 1960

PLATO   *The Laws*
                        Tr. A. E. Taylor
                        London and New York, 1960
                        The Republic
                        Tr. A. D. Lindsay
                        London and New York, 1935

PRICKETT, FREDERICK   *The History and Antiquities of Highgate, Middlesex*
                        London, 1842

PUGIN, A. W. N.   *Contrasts, or a Parallel between the Noble Edifices
                        of the Fourteenth and Fifteenth Centuries and Similar
                        Buildings of the Present Day*
                        London, 1836

QUENNELL, PETER   See MAYHEW, HENRY

RASMUSSEN, STEEN EILER *Towns and Buildings*
                        Liverpool, 1951

ROSENAU, HELEN   *The Ideal City in its Architectural Evolution*
                        London, 1959

ROXAN, DAVID, and   *The Jackdaw of Linz.* The story of Hitler's
WANSTALL, KEN   art thefts
                        London, 1964

RUSKIN, JOHN   *The Seven Lamps of Architecture* and
The Stones of Venice
Various editions

RYAN, A. P.   Article in *The Times*
of 15th February, 1968

SITTE, CAMILLO   *City Planning According to Artistic Principles*
Tr. G. R. Collins and C. C. Collins
London and New York, 1965

SPENGLER, OSWALD   *The Decline of the West*
Tr. C. F. Atkinson
London, 1934

STEWART, CECIL   *A Prospect of Cities*
London, 1952
*Early Christian, Byzantine and
Romanesque Architecture*
London, 1954

SYMONS, LESLIE   *Land Use in Northern Ireland*
(Editor)   Part of the Land Utilization Survey of
Northern Ireland
London, 1963

TAYLOR, NICHOLAS (*et al.*)   Article 'The Failure of Housing' in *The
Architectural Review*, Vol. CXLII, November, 1967

TOYNBEE, ARNOLD   *Cities of Destiny*
(Editor)   London, 1967

VOLK UND REICH VERLAG   *Neue Deutsche Baukunst*
Berlin, 1941

WILKES, LYALL and   *Tyneside Classical. The Newcastle of Grainger,*
DODDS, GORDON   *Dobson and Clayton*
London, 1964

WYCHERLEY, R. E.   *How the Greeks Built Cities*
London, 1962

INDEX